USA TODAY'S DEBATE: VOICES AND PERSPECTIVES

LEGALIZED GAMBLING

Revenue Boom or Social Bust?

Matt Doeden

Twenty-First Century Books · Minneapolis

Twenty-First Century Books
A division of Lerner Publishing Group, Inc.
241 First Avenue North
Minneapolis, MN 55401 U.S.A.

Website address: www.lernerbooks.com

The publisher wishes to thank Ben Nussbaum and Phil Pruitt of USA TODAY for their help in preparing this book.

Library of Congress Cataloging-in-Publication Data

Doeden, Matt.
    Legalized gambling : revenue boom or social bust? / by Matt Doeden.
       p. cm. — (USA today's debate: voices and perspectives)
    Includes bibliographical references and index.
    ISBN: 978-0-7613-5114-6 (lib. bdg. : alk. paper)
    1. Gambling—United States. 2. Gambling—Law and legislation—United States. I. Title.
HV6715.D62 2010
363.4'20973—dc22   2009020573

Manufactured in the United States of America
1 – DP – 12/15/09

CONTENTS

INTRODUCTION

The Legalized Gambling Debate

MILLIONS OF NEW YORKERS LOVE TO PLAY THE lottery. The state of New York sponsors dozens of lottery games, from giant jackpot games such as Mega Millions to video lottery games to instant scratch-off games. A single lottery ticket can cost as little as one dollar or as much as thirty dollars.

Each year, the New York lottery raises billions of dollars. More than 30 percent of that money goes to fund education in the state. That's more than two billion dollars per year, or about 5 percent of the state's total education budget. The money helps pay for teachers, books, and more. The lottery helps fund college scholarships for exceptional students. Lottery profits make a big difference in the education of New York's youth.

Newspapers and TV programs regularly feature stories about lottery winners, telling how the money improves winners' lives. But critics argue that the news often ignores the darker side of the lottery. Many players cannot really afford to play. And for a

Left: Spectators gather in front of the ABC studio in New York City to watch the Mega Millions lottery draw on March 6, 2007. The prize for this draw was a record-breaking $370 million.

small percentage of players, the urge to gamble becomes an addiction.

That was the case with Annie Donnelly of Farmingville, New York. Donnelly was a bookkeeper at a doctor's office. She was in charge of keeping the office's finances in order. But Donnelly had a secret. She was addicted to the lottery. She couldn't control her habit, and soon she couldn't afford it either. So in 2002, she started to embezzle from her employer (steal money entrusted to her). She wrote checks from her employer to herself and cashed

Above: Annie Donnelly spent more than two million dollars on lottery tickets and scratch-off games.

them. Since she kept the books, she reasoned that nobody would notice the missing money.

At first, she was right. She stole more than forty thousand dollars from the office, and nobody noticed. The stolen money fueled her addiction—the urge to gamble grew and grew. On some days, she spent more than six thousand dollars on lottery tickets and scratch-off games. Even when she scored a twenty-five-thousand-dollar jackpot, she poured it right back into lottery tickets. She couldn't get enough.

By 2005 Donnelly's addiction had spun completely out of control. That year she stole more than $1.3 million from her employer. Over three and a half years, she had embezzled about $2.3 million. Her employer's checks began to bounce. She had emptied the accounts. The banks alerted the doctor's office, and soon Donnelly's secret was out. Her employer fired her, and police arrested her in June 2006.

Even Donnelly's husband had been in the dark about her addiction. "I had no idea," Scott Donnelly said. "She was a great mother, she was a great wife, but she had a problem. . . . I guess she thought she'd find a pot of gold at the end of the rainbow and live happily ever after."

Stealing money for gambling is all too common among compulsive gamblers. But the scale of Donnelly's addiction was shocking. New York's Suffolk County assistant district attorney Donna M. Planty said, "The irony is the total amount of money she stole is more than she would have won if she hit the lottery. When I first got the case, I said, 'You've got to be kidding.' "

It was no joking matter, however. In August 2006, Donnelly pled guilty to second-degree grand larceny. Grand larceny is theft on a large scale. The court sentenced her to between four and twelve years in prison. "Tell me how you're helping me!" Donnelly screamed at the judge during her sentencing. "So put me upstate [in prison]. But you know what? When I come out, I'm still going to have a [gambling] problem." She went on to threaten suicide.

BOILING DOWN THE DEBATE

For many people, the lottery and other forms of gambling are just innocent pastimes. For a dollar or two, anyone can dream of winning

USA TODAY Snapshots®

Instant winners ... and losers

Scratch-off lottery ticket sales:
(in billions)

5.2   1990
11.5   1995
15.5   2000
28.3   2006

Source: 2007 World Lottery Almanac

By David Stuckey and Karl Gelles, USA TODAY, 2008

millions. Players at casinos enjoy the thrill of slot machines and games such as blackjack and poker. Most play for fun and leave when they've spent their limit or get tired of playing. But for a small percentage of gamblers, it's not that easy. For addicts such as Annie Donnelly, gambling is a compulsion. It can ruin lives and livelihoods.

The danger of compulsive gambling is just one aspect of the ongoing debate about legalized gambling. This debate has stretched over a wide variety of areas, from Indian gaming to sports betting to gambling's newest frontier, the Internet.

Each area of the debate has its own set of issues and arguments. But a few basic themes recur. Opponents of expanding and legalizing gambling tend to pose arguments in three general categories: moral objections, economic objections, and concerns over compulsive behavior.

Moral arguments are especially common among religious groups

Above: Iraqi Muslims gamble on a dice game on the holiday of Eid al-Fitr, which ends the holy month of Ramadan. Some Muslims avoid gambling only during religious holidays, while others refuse to gamble at all.

Above: The text of the Bible does not prohibit gambling directly. However, many Christians claim that gambling encourages greed and envy, which the Bible condemns.

fighting against gambling. The Quran, the holy book of Islam, bans gambling. Many Christians claim that the Bible opposes gambling as well. They say that gambling is a form of greed and that it has no place in a moral society. Many Buddhists, meanwhile, believe that gambling can cause a person to lose self-control—an important principle of Buddhism.

The counterarguments to moral objections are simple. Supporters of legalized gambling say morality is relative. In other words, what one person considers moral behavior, another might consider immoral. Those who consider gambling immoral should not participate. One person's morality should not be forced upon another person. Another moral counterargument is that the Judeo-Christian Bible never specifically prohibits gambling. Several passages speak out against greed or the love of money, but not gambling specifically.

The Roman Catholic Church does not consider gambling sinful. According to the Catechism (teachings) of the Catholic Church, "Games of chance (card games, etc.) or wagers are not in themselves contrary to justice. They become morally unacceptable when they deprive someone of what is necessary to provide for his needs and those of others. The passion for gambling risks becoming an enslavement."

The second main objection to legalized gambling is an economic one. To gamble is to bet money or property on an uncertain outcome. Gambling moves money from one owner to another. For every winner, there are multiple losers.

In many cases, gamblers are people who cannot afford

Above: Many elderly people enjoy gambling. Casinos and other gambling sites give them a place to meet friends and play games. But gambling can also cause financial problems for retired people who have a limited amount of money to support themselves.

to gamble. One study showed that, in terms of income percentage, the poor spend 2.5 times more on gambling than the rich or the middle class do. More than a quarter of low-income gamblers claim to gamble in order to get rich. These gamblers may see gambling as the only way out of poverty. But more often than not, gambling only worsens financial problems. Gambling, some argue, can ultimately lead to higher crime rates. As increasingly desperate people scramble to survive, some turn to stealing and other illegal acts.

Closely related to the economic objection is the concern about compulsive gambling. Some people lack the self-control needed to limit their gambling. As they lose, they bet more and more—a behavior called chasing losses. The compulsive gambler, when losing, insists that he or she has to keep gambling to break even. Compulsive gamblers who are winning insist that they must keep gambling because they're on a hot streak. Some people believe that the compulsion to gamble is an addiction similar to alcohol or drug addiction.

The counterarguments to the economic objection and the concern over compulsive gamblers are similar. Supporters of legalized gambling concede that the activity is harmful to some. But they also believe that in a free society, people should be

Above: Protesters demonstrate against the proposed opening of a dozen new casinos in Kentucky in 2008.

able to spend their money as they please. A 2004 poll by the American Gaming Association (AGA) revealed that 86 percent of U.S. adults believe that they should have the right to gamble with their own money if they choose to do so. The faults of some should not take away the rights of everyone else. Furthermore, supporters say, legalizing and regulating gambling makes people less likely to turn to illegal wagering, such as with sports bookies. (Bookies, or bookmakers, are people who calculate odds, take bets, and pay winnings.) Because illegal gambling is unsupervised, it is rife with cheating. Ultimately, many argue, a fully regulated system better protects gamblers.

THE ROLE OF GOVERNMENT

What role should state and federal governments play in gambling? A government may take one of four positions:

1. Prohibition
2. Tolerance
3. Regulation
4. Operation

The first possible role is prohibition. A government adopting this role simply outlaws gambling in some or all of its forms.

In the role of tolerance, the government allows private and/or public gambling and makes no effort to control it. This is the most passive role a government can take. A tolerant government need not spend resources to enforce antigambling laws, but it also has no say in the fairness of gaming operations.

A government in the regulation role sets the laws and standards that legal gambling must follow. States may allow some forms of gambling and outlaw others. For example, games of skill may be legal, while games of chance are illegal—or vice versa. Or a government may allow widespread gambling but with strict standards and safeguards. Governments may also set up special regulatory bodies, such as the Nevada Gaming Control Board, to oversee gaming activities.

The final possible role of government is active participation, or operation. This is the

Above: During a 2000 state legislative session, Steve DuCharme of the Nevada Gaming Control Board speaks on the rise of Internet gambling.

role adopted by states that run lotteries, racetracks, and other gambling endeavors. Rather than sitting back and setting standards for private gaming companies, the states take control of gaming. This stance ensures maximum fairness—although even state-sponsored gambling businesses can be corrupt. But this role also has a number of sharp critics. They claim that governments have no business being involved in gambling. Critics may believe that gaming should be a private industry or that it should be outlawed altogether.

The debate over the legalization and expansion of gambling is a passionate one. It weighs the freedom of the individual over the greater good of society. It poses many questions with no black-and-white answers. Do the benefits of legalized gambling outweigh the costs? Whom should the law protect? Should it protect the freedom of the majority to make their own choices? Or should it protect the minority from themselves?

CHAPTER ONE

Historical Perspective: Gambling and the Law

HOW LONG HAVE PEOPLE BEEN GAMBLING? Gambling may be older than historians can track. It pervaded almost every ancient society on record. The desire to gamble may in fact be innate to humans.

A 2005 Duke University study showed that our evolutionary cousins share our desire to gamble. The study tested macaque monkeys. To reward the monkeys for completing various tasks, researchers gave the monkeys a choice of two targets, each of which dispensed an amount of juice. One target always released the same measure of juice. The second target released a varying amount. Usually, the second target released less juice than the first target. And the average amount released by the second target was less than that of the first target. But once in a while, a monkey could hit the jackpot and get a large serving. Despite the risk of getting less juice, the monkeys more frequently chose the variable target. At its core,

Left: This Greek vase from the 500s B.C. shows mythological heroes Achilles and Ajax gambling with dice. Archaeologists have unearthed dice made as early as 5000 B.C.

Above: Researchers used macaque monkeys like these in their gambling study.

this was a gambling behavior. The monkeys were willing to risk getting a small amount of juice in the hopes of getting lucky. Researcher Michael Platt explained:

> Basically these monkeys really liked to gamble. There was something intrinsically rewarding about choosing a target that offered a variable juice reward, as if the variability in rewards that they experienced was in itself rewarding. . . . If [the monkeys] got a big reward one time on the risky choice, but then continued to get small rewards, they would keep going back as if they were searching or waiting or hoping to get that big payoff. It seemed very, very similar to the experience of people who are compulsive gamblers. While it's always dangerous to anthropomorphize [attribute human characteristics to animals], it seemed as if these monkeys got a high out of getting a big reward that obliterated [erased] any memory of all the losses that they would experience following that big reward.

This story tells us that the desire to gamble may be an inborn trait in primates (a group of animals that includes monkeys and human beings). If that's the case, should laws protect our right to follow that desire? Or should they protect us from ourselves?

GAMBLING IN THE ANCIENT WORLD

Gambling was as pervasive in the ancient world as it is in the modern one. So was the impact of gambling on society.

Gambling in ancient Egypt, for example, was widespread. Games of chance, often played with dice, were a favorite pastime. And just as in modern times, these games had winners and losers. Ancient accounts tell of Egyptians working off their gambling debts in stone quarries. In fact, archaeologists think that some of the people who labored to build Egypt's great pyramids may have been compulsive gamblers working off debts.

The Egyptian urge to gamble wasn't limited to the common people. Pharaohs (kings) who died were sometimes entombed with their "lucky" dice at their side. It's no surprise that some of the dice discovered with the mummified kings were weighted, or "fixed," to favor certain outcomes. After all, who would question an all-power-ful pharaoh about the fairness of his dice? The fixed dice suggest that as long as people have been gambling, they have also been trying to cheat.

Gambling was also central to the culture

Above: Archaeologists discovered these dice at a site in India. They were made around 2500 B.C.

Above: This Chinese statue from the A.D. 100s shows two people playing Liubo, an ancient dice game played on a game board.

of ancient China. Almost every major city in ancient China had one or more gambling houses. The Chinese wagered on a wide range of games and events. They played a lottery that used cards painted with animal pictures. People commonly wagered upon games of skill, such as the board game Go. People also avidly bet on animal fights. Cricket fights were very popular, and they remain so in modern times.

The ancient Greeks were avid gamblers too. Even their gods were gamblers. One Greek legend says that the god Zeus won control of the heavens by casting lots, a popular ancient form of gambling, with the gods Poseidon and Hades. Poseidon won the sea, and Hades won the underworld. If gambling was good enough for the gods, it was good enough for the Greek people as well. Greek gamblers prayed to their patron, the god Hermes, for good fortune.

The culture of the Roman Empire that followed was based on Greek ideals, including the love of gambling. The Romans

Above: Spectators in the Roman Colosseum placed bets on gladiators, who fought different kinds of animals—and sometimes one another—in deadly battles.

were notorious for their betting—on everything from dice games to bloody battles in the Colosseum. The early Romans viewed life itself as a game of chance. Roman leader Julius Caesar illustrated that mind-set when, in 41 B.C., he exclaimed, "Alea iacta est" (The die has been cast) as he sent his armies into battle. Once he'd made a decision, he left the results to chance. With a worldview like that, it's little wonder many ancient Romans prayed to Fortuna, the goddess of luck.

Ancient gambling was not unique to these large civilizations. Wagering appeared almost everywhere in some form. For example, the Christian Bible tells many stories about casting lots

> ## Gaming is the mother of lies and perjuries.
>
> **—JOHN OF SALISBURY,**
> A TWELFTH-CENTURY AUTHOR AND CATHOLIC BISHOP

and other forms of gambling. Governments rarely regulated gambling in the ancient world. Those who piled up gambling debt risked punishment from their creditors. And cheats might pay with their lives if discovered. But for centuries, gambling laws were few and far between.

GAMBLING IN
COLONIAL AMERICA

When Europeans began to explore the Americas in the late 1400s and early 1500s, they brought gambling with them. Christopher Columbus's crew gambled aboard their ships with dice and playing cards. But Columbus and other explorers did not introduce the pastime to the Native Americans they met. They discovered that gambling was already well established among the people they called Indians. Native Americans avidly wagered on events such as athletic competitions. Losers often lost everything they owned. European explorers and Native Americans had little in common, but they all loved to gamble.

Across Europe and in European colonies, including

Below: In 1835 George Catlin painted this picture of hundreds of Choctaw men playing a Native American ball game.

Above: European men gamble with dice for coins and jewelry in a woodcut from the 1500s.

those in North America, governments usually took a hands-off approach to gambling. But some argued that gambling led to an immoral society. The first serious pushes toward making gambling illegal were under way. Laws criminalizing various types of gambling appeared in England in 1542 and again in 1665. A law against lotteries followed in 1698. These laws were limited and short-lived. But they showed that moral and legal objections to gambling were growing.

While some fought for laws to ban gambling, others promoted it as a way to fund English colonies in North America. Captain John Smith played an instrumental role in settling the Jamestown colony in present-day Virginia. When the colony experienced financial troubles, Smith got permission from King James to hold lotteries in London to raise money.

The French also got in on the lottery game. In 1729 France started a royal lottery. Only owners of the nation's

Above: A French nobleman oversees a local lottery held in Paris in the early 1700s to raise money for a new church.

municipal bonds could take part. (A bond is an investment in which citizens loan a government money with a promised rate of return.) France hoped the lottery would increase bond sales. However, the French lottery was badly flawed. Each bond entitled the holder to buy one ticket. The price of the bond determined the price of the ticket. So a ten thousand–franc bondholder paid one hundred times more for a lottery ticket than a one hundred–franc bondholder did. But both tickets held the same chance of winning the prize. A team of bondholders realized that by buying massive amounts of the cheapest bonds—and the cheapest tickets—they could tip the odds strongly in their favor. The French government discontinued the lottery a year later.

During the mid-1700s, tensions between Great Britain and France were high. The British colonies in North America were concerned about French attack, since France also had colonies in

North America. So some of the colonies held lotteries, using the proceeds to buy cannons and fortifications. During the French and Indian War (1754–1763), a lottery furnished money to buy supplies for volunteer British colonial troops.

All thirteen original British colonies supported fund-raising lotteries at some point. However, many colonial Americans despised gambling. Religious settlers such as the Puritans argued that gambling undermined the work ethic—the idea that a person's wealth should come from hard work. The legislature of colonial Massachusetts labeled gambling devices such as cards and dice to be the devil's playthings.

EARLY UNITED STATES

The young U.S. government declared independence from Great Britain in 1776. U.S. leaders knew that they needed money to pay for a war against the powerful British military. But raising money via taxes was not an option, considering the strong sentiment against taxation among the colonists. The

and bone knives and forks, buckles and buttons, with a variety of cutlary, Manchester, and other goods. Thctf.

S C H E M E

Of a LOTTERY to be set up in PHILADEL-PHIA, for the benefit of the New-Jersey College, to consist of 8000 tickets, at Thirty Shillings each, 2152 of which to be fortunate.

Number of Prizes.		Value of each. l.		Total Value. l.
1	of	500	is	500
2	of	250	are	500
9	of	100	are	900
20	of	50	are	1000
40	of	20	are	800
200	of	10	are	2000
1880	of	2l. 10s.	are	4700
		First drawn		40
		Last drawn		60
Prizes	2152			
Blanks	5848			l. 10500

8000 Tickets, at 30s. each, is 12000 l.
From which deduct 12 and a half per Cent. is   1500
                                                   l. 12000

The drawing to begin on the 23d day of April next, or sooner, if sooner full, of which timely notice will be given, that such adventurers as choose to be present, may see the tickets put into the boxes.

We hope those who wish well to the education of the rising generation will encourage the design; which is to furnish the youth with all useful learning, and at the same time to instil into their minds the principles of morality and piety.

The following persons are appointed managers of the lottery, viz. William Branson, George Spafford, Samuel Smith, Samuel Hazard, William Shippen, Joseph Redman, Andrew Read, and William Patterson, in Pennsylvania; and James Hude, James Nelson, and Samuel Woodruff, in the Jerseys; who are to give bond, and be on oath, for the faithful performance of their trust.

Prizes not demanded within six months after the drawing, to be deem'd as generously given to the use of said college, and not to be demanded afterwards, but applied accordingly.

The tickets will begin to be sold by the managers at their respective dwellings, on the first day of January. And also by Peter Vanbrugh Levingston, and William Peartree Smith, in New-York.

VEry good Jesuit's Bark to be sold by John Inglis, at his store, on Hamilton's Wharff.

Just imported, and to be sold by
BENJAMIN RAWLE,
Next door but one to the Ferry-house, in Water-street, WEst India rum, melasses, coffee, cocoa, and cases of bottles.

Above: Benjamin Franklin printed this ad for a lottery in a 1749 issue of the *Pennsylvania Gazette.*

> **" Our Founding Fathers were greatly aided by a lottery, and Americans haven't stopped gambling since. "**
>
> —**DANNY SHERIDAN,** SPORTS GAMBLING EXPERT
> ⓒ USA TODAY · JANUARY 30, 2009

colonists were rebelling against British rule largely because of excessive taxation. The U.S. government's answer to this dilemma was a voluntary tax—a lottery. The lottery was a failure. It didn't even raise enough money to pay the prize. But it showed that the young nation considered lotteries an important source of revenue.

The founders of the United States struggled with the same basic questions about gambling that modern lawmakers face. Many of the founders recognized gambling as a destructive force in society. They were unsure that state-sponsored lotteries were a good idea. But they had established the United States as a free country, recognizing the right of white men to life, liberty, and the pursuit of happiness. The idea of telling adult citizens that they could not gamble did not sit well with many founders.

Thomas Jefferson, the author of the Declaration of Independence, pondered the benefits and drawbacks of gambling. He wrote:

> If we consider games of chance immoral, then every pursuit of human industry is immoral; for there is not a single one that is not subject to chance, not one wherein you do not risk a loss for the chance of some gain. . . . These, then, are games of chance . . . and every one has a natural right to choose for his pursuit such one of them as he thinks most likely to furnish him subsistence. . . .

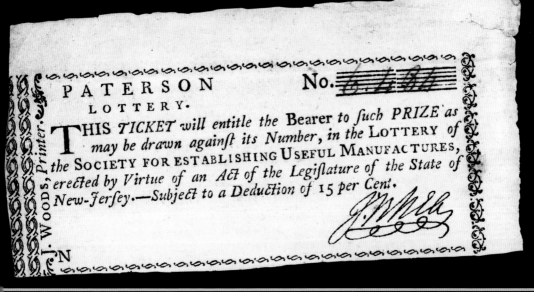

PATERSON LOTTERY.

No.

THIS TICKET will entitle the Bearer to such PRIZE as may be drawn against its Number, in the LOTTERY of the SOCIETY FOR ESTABLISHING USEFUL MANUFACTURES, erected by Virtue of an Act of the Legislature of the State of New-Jersey.—Subject to a Deduction of 15 per Cent.

J. WOODS, Printer.

Above: This 1791 lottery ticket was part of a New Jersey state fund-raiser. The money collected during this lottery went to the Society for Establishing Useful Manufactures, which encouraged industrial development in the state.

But there are some [games of chance] which produce nothing, and endanger the well-being of the individuals engaged in them or of others depending on them.... Society... step[s] in to protect the family and the party himself.

Public lotteries remained important to the United States through the early 1800s, despite widespread corruption and scandal among lottery administrators. Lotteries brought needed revenue to state and local governments. Proceeds paid for roads and bridges and filled state treasuries. Private lotteries were even more widespread. They helped fund the building of schools and churches.

The tide turned in 1829, when President Andrew Jackson took office. Jackson himself was a gambler. He favored horse racing. But that did not stop him from leading a crusade against state-sponsored gambling. Yet his efforts did not meet with immediate results. In 1832 the United States held more than four hundred state-sponsored lotteries. Combined, the lotteries sold about sixty-six million dollars worth of tickets. That figure was more than five times the total federal budget for 1832. But by the mid-1800s, only three states still sponsored lotteries.

Other forms of gambling quickly filled the void. Riverboat casinos emerged, and wagering on horse races grew more popular. Despite the objections of a vocal minority, Americans clearly liked gambling. As far as most were concerned, they could do as they pleased with their money. The government had no place telling them otherwise.

THE WILD WEST

Unregulated gambling thrived in the western United States in the mid-1800s. After John Marshall discovered gold in California in 1848, tens of thousands of men and women flocked west to seek their fortunes. While many failed to find gold, others struck it rich. The combination of a population boom, sudden wealth, and a general lack of law enforcement was the perfect recipe for a rapid increase in gambling.

Gold seekers made up the first wave of westward migrants. Other waves soon followed. These included not only miners but also professional gamblers eager to fleece the miners. From poker to dice games, gambling had become so common so quickly that California lawmakers wanted a piece of the action. In 1849 California recognized gambling as a legal profession. By legalizing the activity, California could tax the gamblers' incomes.

Still, gambling in the Wild West was often a rough-and-tumble affair. Gamblers took their lives into their own hands. A cheat or even a suspected cheat could easily end up with a black eye—or a bullet to the brain. Big winners were vulnerable to robbery. Everyone risked being cheated, because the games were entirely unregulated. For some professional gamblers, the Wild West was a paradise. But for others,

Above: This illustration shows gamblers playing faro, a card game, in a California casino in the mid-1800s.

gambling was a quick ticket to poverty or the grave.

THE 1900S

The late 1800s and early 1900s saw a sharp antigambling swing in public opinion. The swing was part of a widespread temperance movement, which discouraged excess of any kind. Temperance leaders specifically argued that drinking liquor led to a host of social ills. The Eighteenth Amendment to the U.S. Constitution, passed in 1919, outlawed the manufacture, sale, and transport of alcoholic beverages. This law ushered in the Prohibition era. Many Prohibitionists believed gambling was dangerous to society too, so many antigambling laws soon followed.

Prohibition was a disaster. Many people simply ignored the law, and enforcement was spotty. It also opened a whole new crime front, with bootleggers illegally providing liquor and forming large organized crime syndicates. Prohibition was wildly unpopular among average Americans, who did not want the government telling them what they could and could not do.

The United States repealed the Prohibition law in 1933. Around the same time, many states began to realize that people were going to gamble regardless of the law. It was better, some states decided, to regulate gambling and get a cut of the revenue than to waste resources trying to prohibit gambling.

To satisfy the public hunger for gambling and to stem the tide of illegal wagering, lawmakers in many states found a compromise: horse racing. The sport had been popular for more than a century, especially in the eastern United States. Its great popularity had protected horse racing and betting from Prohibition-era antigambling laws. Lawmakers reasoned that because the breeding, raising, and selling of horses was

Above: In 1938 gamblers set an all-time betting record at the "Match of the Century" between champion horses Seabiscuit *(above)* and War Admiral. Seabiscuit beat War Admiral, becoming not only a gambler's dream but also a symbol of hope for the underdog.

already a major industry, more legal horse racing could be a great economic stimulus. As new private, state-sanctioned tracks sprang up around the nation, the sport's popularity grew to new heights. Racetracks thrived, even during the dark days of the Great Depression (1929–1942). Wagering, it seemed, was one luxury that many Americans could not live without.

Racetracks continued to do well through the 1900s. For many Americans, racetracks were the only easy and legal places to gamble.

October 10, 1991

Hawthorne celebrates 100th year

From the Pages of USA TODAY   Hawthorne Race Course, one of the USA's oldest Thoroughbred facilities, today opens its autumn meeting amid the fanfare of the track's 100th anniversary. Racing debuted at the southwest Chicago track May 20, 1891, under the ownership of Thomas F. Carey. The Carey family maintains a controlling interest.

"When (the track) burned in 1978, we had very little insurance," says president and general manager Thomas Carey, grandson of the founder. "We were, for all practical purposes, out of business." But Hawthorne reopened and, 13 years later, is part of what Carey views as an ongoing rejuvenation of Chicago-area racing.

Only four other tracks have operated longer than Hawthorne - Saratoga (Saratoga Springs, N.Y., 1863); Pimlico (Baltimore, 1870); Fair Grounds (New Orleans, 1872); and Churchill Downs (Louisville, 1874). Laurel (Md.) Race Course begins its 80th year today.

—Steve Woodward and Pohla Smith

Above: Gamblers at a betting hall in Las Vegas, Nevada, place bets on horse races around the United States in 1939.

State-sponsored lotteries began to reappear in the 1960s. Many states took advantage of the fact that the federal government left gambling laws largely up to the individual states. The end result was that gambling laws varied widely from state to state. While some states such as Nevada embraced gambling in nearly all its forms, others shunned it. Most states, however, fell somewhere in the middle. They applied their own laws and logic to gambling legislation.

The gambling landscape changed again in the late 1980s.

In 1988 Congress passed the Indian Gaming Regulatory Act (IGRA). The act acknowledged the right of Native Americans to conduct gaming activities on tribal lands. Suddenly, gambling venues—mainly casinos—popped up in dozens of states. The casino experience appealed to many Americans. Casinos offered a wide range of games, including slot machines. Gambling on a slot machine was easy, unlike betting on a horse race—which required special knowledge about horses and mathematics.

Las Vegas

Las Vegas got its start as a gambling hot spot in the 1920s and 1930s. When authorities in neighboring California cracked down on illegal gambling clubs in that state, some clubs relocated to Nevada. Many landed in Las Vegas, where gambling laws were lax and enforcement even looser.

By the 1940s, the Las Vegas gambling industry was rolling full steam ahead. Nevada further loosened gambling restrictions, and small gambling clubs grew into huge casinos. Lavish hotels, fancy nightclubs, and world-class entertainment helped bring in tourists. The city's gambling centers, both downtown and southward along Las Vegas Boulevard (the Strip), grew and grew. By 2008 the total revenue of Nevada casinos was about $11.6 billion. Las Vegas casinos earned most of this money.

Above: This 1939 photo of Fremont Street in Las Vegas shows the Overland Hotel and the Northern Club. Opened in 1920, the Northern Club served alcohol and hosted poker and other gambling games despite Prohibition.

Predictably, racetracks suffered. States scrambled to renew interest in horse racing and get people back to the tracks. The most common strategy was to allow casino-style games—usually slot machines—on racetrack grounds. Racing establishments with casino gambling became known as racinos. Racinos did draw people back to the track. But the horse racing often took a backseat to the casino games. U.S. gaming had undergone a massive shift. To the delight of some and the consternation of many, legal gambling was more accessible than ever before.

The gambling boom wasn't limited to casinos and racinos. Other forms of gambling were also taking off—especially state-sponsored lotteries. An old idea was building up a new head of steam. Public lotteries brought in big revenues, which states could use to boost cash-strapped programs. People loved lotteries because they could hope for tens of millions of dollars on

Above: Powerball winner Solomon Jackson Jr. shows off a ceremonial check for his 2009 winnings in the South Carolina Education Lottery.

investments as small as one dollar. Before long, huge multistate lotteries had jackpots exceeding one hundred million dollars.

In the 1990s, just as brick-and-mortar venues for legal gambling were becoming widely available, everything changed again. The dawn of online gaming opened gambling to anyone with a computer, an Internet connection, and a credit card. Suddenly, people could play slot machines, blackjack, poker, or almost any game from the comfort of their own homes. Many early online operations were shady and unregulated. Their patrons were vulnerable to fraud and outright theft. But reputable gaming sites also appeared.

Governments around the world scrambled to deal with the sudden availability of Internet gaming. Some nations, including many in Europe, moved to regulate the games. Others, such as the United States, took steps to outlaw Internet gambling. Many online operations set up shop in countries beyond the reach of governments who wished to outlaw them. International trade law and a wide variety of national business, gambling, and tax laws complicated matters for individual governments trying to control online gambling. Only time will tell how these issues will ultimately resolve.

CHAPTER TWO

Out of Control: Compulsive Gambling

JOSEPH KUPCHIK WAS IN MOST WAYS AN ORDINARY college student. He was studying accounting at a college in Cleveland, Ohio. He loved to play and watch sports. In 2004 Kupchik and his brother John discovered online gambling. They put seventy dollars into an online sportsbook so that they could place small bets on National Football League (NFL) games. The brothers discussed the games to strategize and choose their bets. At first the bets were modest—just enough to encourage the brothers to hone their prediction skills. As the Kupchiks won again and again, the sizes of their bets grew. Soon their investment had grown to sixteen hundred dollars.

John took his half of the winnings and cashed out. But Joseph was hooked. He turned his attention to college basketball—with considerably less success. At one point, Kupchik's savings account had contained

Left: A man plays poker at an online gaming site. Easy access to Internet wagering makes gambling bans difficult for states to enforce.

about seven thousand dollars. But that money quickly disappeared. Soon he had just a few dollars left.

Kupchik was losing more and more money. He reportedly gambled some of his tuition away. Over two days in January 2006, he lost more than eighteen hundred dollars. His football betting gains had long since disappeared. His betting had spun out of control. He had become a compulsive gambler.

No one knows what really happened to Kupchik in the final hours of his life. Had he

Above: Websites such as this one, founded in 1997, offer players poker, casino games, and sports betting.

gone in debt to dangerous people? Or was he so despondent about his financial situation that he felt suicidal?

One thing is certain. On the night of February 11, 2006, Kupchik was stabbed and fell nine stories to his death. Investigators found a note he had written shortly before he died:

> Expectations can either be positive or negative, but rarely am I ever right. Whenever I anticipate an event probably to make my dreams come true, something usually happens where the situation turns into a nightmare.

That note, combined with information about Kupchik's gambling losses, led investigators to rule his death a suicide. (Many of his friends and family members believe someone murdered him.) Regardless of the precise cause, the young man lost his life—and gambling almost certainly played a role.

Kupchik's story is one example among many tragedies wrought by compulsive gambling. Stories such as these lead many to oppose the legalization and expansion of gambling. Opponents say that in the wrong hands, gambling can destroy lives.

WHY DO PEOPLE GAMBLE?

A 1999 study by the National Gambling Impact Study Commission (NGISC) revealed that about 125 million U.S. citizens gamble. Among those, NGISC defines 7.5 million as problem gamblers. The term *problem gamblers* refers to both compulsive gamblers (also called pathological gamblers) and people who gamble above their means.

Above: Gambling can provide emotional excitement that some people find hard to give up.

(In other words, they wager more money than they can afford to lose.) Other studies show that about 5 percent of gamblers fall into the compulsive category.

Why are five out of one hundred gamblers unable to control their betting? To understand why, one must first learn why people gamble in the first place. Surveys turn up a number of reasons for gambling, including:

- To win money
- For entertainment and excitement
- To socialize
- As a distraction from day-to-day life
- To support charitable causes
- As a hobby

Compulsive gamblers typically list the first two reasons for their behavior. Often, compulsive gamblers believe their fortune is just around the corner. When asked how much money they have won or lost, they tend to sugarcoat the truth. A compulsive gambler who has won a little will claim to be a big winner. A player

Characteristics of a Compulsive Gambler

According to Gamblers Anonymous, most compulsive gamblers share a few traits.
1. The inability or unwillingness to accept reality
2. Emotional insecurity
3. Immaturity
4. The need to feel in control

who has lost a little may claim to be even. And big losers may minimize their losses. Is this lying or an inability to honestly assess a situation?

Other forms of self-delusion may contribute to compulsive gambling. Countless gamblers claim to have "systems" that allow them to beat the odds. For example, in the game of roulette, in which players bet on the roll of a ball into a spinning wheel with red and black numbers, chance determines the outcome. But many players believe they have discovered a way to predict where the ball will land. For example, a player may believe that if the ball has landed on red a certain number of times in a row, the wheel must be "due" for a black result.

This reasoning is flawed. Players subscribing to such systems don't understand—or

Above: In roulette, players can bet that the ball will roll into a pocket of a certain color, a certain number, a range of numbers, or an odd or even number.

Above: A member of an antigambling group in Omaha, Nebraska, speaks about his gambling problem at a news conference. As a student at the University of Nebraska–Lincoln, he spent days at a time gambling in casinos instead of studying.

don't want to believe—that every spin of the wheel is an independent event. The wheel does not know what the last several results have been. The odds of a red result are exactly the same on every spin. Basing a wager on past spins is no more effective than flipping a coin to choose a bet. But compulsive gamblers often con themselves into believing they've found a secret edge.

Gambling for excitement is also common among compulsives. The roll of the dice, spin of the wheel, or turn of the card is an exciting, suspenseful moment. The body's adrenal glands release the hormone adrenaline (also called epinephrine) in threatening or exciting situations. Many players comment on the "adrenaline rush" they get from placing a large wager or scoring a big win. Compulsives may continue to gamble as a means of chasing the next adrenaline rush. In pursuit of that high, they lose control of their behavior.

THE DAMAGE CAUSED BY COMPULSIVE GAMBLING

Compulsive gambling can ruin lives, both economically and socially. Compulsive gamblers can quickly burn through their savings. They may constantly ask to borrow money from friends or family. Meanwhile, many compulsives go to great lengths to hide their financial ruin. They believe that a hot streak is just around the corner and that their problems will soon be solved.

The need to gamble pushes some compulsives to break the law. In a poll of Gamblers Anonymous (GA) members, more than half admitted to having stolen money to feed their obsession.

Not all compulsive gamblers are money losers. In the card game poker, for example, a skilled player can make money consistently. Top players can even make a profession of the game. But even winning players

Above: Art Schlichter lost a promising career in professional football to compulsive gambling. In 1995 a judge sentenced him to prison for stealing money to support his habit. His desire to gamble was so strong that he illegally smuggled a phone into his cell to place bets.

can suffer damage from compulsive gambling. Their play may be a financial boon, but it can also be a social bust. If they become obsessed with gambling, they may neglect friends, family, and even their health.

Compulsive gamblers also face serious health concerns.

According to the National Council on Problem Gambling (NCPG), young people who gamble are 50 percent more likely than non-gamblers to binge on alcohol and 75 percent more likely to smoke marijuana. Compulsives often eat poorly and get little exercise.

Am I a Problem Gambler?

This list of questions comes from the National Council on Problem Gambling. According to NCPG, anyone who answers yes to one or more of these questions may have a problem and should consider seeking help.

1. Have you often gambled longer than you had planned?
2. Have you often gambled until your last dollar was gone?
3. Have thoughts of gambling caused you to lose sleep?
4. Have you used your income or savings to gamble while letting bills go unpaid?
5. Have you made repeated, unsuccessful attempts to stop gambling?
6. Have you broken the law or considered breaking the law to finance your gambling?
7. Have you borrowed money to finance your gambling?
8. Have you felt depressed or suicidal because of your gambling losses?
9. Have you been remorseful after gambling?
10. Have you gambled to get money to meet your financial obligations?

Compulsive gambling can lead to a wide range of damaging behaviors. Another study revealed some shocking statistics about recovering gambling addicts. Of those surveyed, 40 percent cited gambling as the reason for having lost a job, while 22 percent cited gambling as a reason for a divorce. Other numbers were even more troubling: 23 percent admitted to alcoholism and 26 percent to compulsive overeating. A shocking 63 percent had contemplated suicide, while 79 percent admitted to having wanted to die at some point. Bankruptcy rates among problem gamblers were also higher than those among the rest of the population.

The bottom line, some say, is that gambling creates significant societal problems as well as personal ones. The University of Chicago's National Opinion Research Center (NORC) esti-mated that the treatment and fallout of problem gambling costs society more than five billion dollars per year. Opponents of legalized gambling say such figures show that gambling does far more harm than good to society.

Supporters of legalized gambling say that the numbers used by antigambling groups are largely guesswork. Supporters also claim that antigambling groups exaggerate many figures. They see

USA TODAY Snapshots®

Medical events threaten financial health

Of the more than 1.45 million families in the USA who filed for bankruptcy[1], 54.5% blamed medical problems. Most frequently cited reasons:

Illness or injury	28%
Birth/addition of new family member	8%
Death in family	8%
Alcohol or drug addiction	3%
Uncontrolled gambling	1%

1 – Data collected in 2001. Many people gave more than one reason. Families includes filers, non-filers and children.
Source: Health Affairs, February 2005

By Ashley Burrell and Marcy E. Mullins, USA TODAY, 2005

compulsive gambling as a small problem easily addressed by proper regulation and treatment.

IS COMPULSIVE GAMBLING A DISEASE?

Debate rages over how to classify problem gamblers. Is compulsive gambling a disease? Is it an addiction similar to a drug or an alcohol addiction?

Many argue that the urge to gamble is a true addiction and that compulsives have little control over their behavior. They claim that many compulsives are addicted to the adrenaline rush they get when they gamble—and especially when they win.

Some studies suggest that there may indeed be a chemical component to—and a chemical treatment for—problem gambling. For example, a study published in the February 2006 issue of the *American Journal of Psychiatry* showed that a drug called nalmefene could benefit compulsive gamblers. Doctors normally use nalmefene

Above: Jean Holthaus, president of the Kansas Coalition on Problem Gambling, displays literature aimed at helping compulsive gamblers.

to treat alcohol and drug dependence. Nalmefene's ability to help some problem gamblers suggests that compulsive gambling is a form of chemical addiction.

Others argue that addictions are the result of a chemical dependence and that gambling does not fall into that category. They point out that a gambler is not putting a chemical into his or her body, as does an alcoholic or an abuser of drugs. For this reason, they believe that compulsive gambling is really more a lack of willpower rather than a chemical dependence. The American Psychiatric Association (APA) agrees. In 1980 the APA officially recognized problem gambling as an "impulse control disorder." People with such disorders repeatedly perform an act (such as gambling) without regard for its potential harm. So the APA does not consider compulsive gambling an addiction.

HELP FOR COMPULSIVE GAMBLERS

Several groups offer help to compulsive gamblers. One is Gamblers Anonymous. GA is based on Alcoholics Anonymous, the highly successful support system for alcoholics. GA includes a social support network for recovering gambling addicts, as well as a recovery program that helps addicts break their patterns of destructive behavior. Many other programs help compulsive

> ❝ **[There is] emerging evidence that gambling, once thought to be a problem with moral integrity, is instead a problem in brain biology and can be treated successfully.** ❞
>
> **—ROBERT FREEDMAN,**
> EDITOR IN CHIEF, *AMERICAN JOURNAL OF PSYCHIATRY,* 2006

> ❝ **I get bored and lonely and sad. I talk myself into going down to the casinos. My mind tricks me into thinking I can win. But then I can't leave until I've lost everything.** ❞

—SCOTT JONES,
A PROBLEM GAMBLER ON NEW JERSEY'S SELF-EXCLUSION LIST, 2009

gamblers too, including some operated by state governments. Most of these programs follow a similar strategy: helping problem gamblers learn to eliminate gambling behavior. The resources such programs offer can save lives, families, and livelihoods.

But some people question the effectiveness of such programs. They have high dropout rates. One study showed that only 8 percent of those attending GA meetings had managed to go a full year without wagering. Critics of GA in particular say that abstinence (complete avoidance) is not the ideal strategy for many problem gamblers because it's too hard to sustain. Instead,

Above: A North Carolina man tells his story of gambling addiction at a Gamblers Anonymous meeting in 2005.

Above: The Seneca Niagara Casino in New York offers a self-exclusion policy and counseling opportunities for problem gamblers.

they say controlled betting should be the goal because it brings better long-term results. Controlled betting programs help problem gamblers modify their behavior and learn to control their impulses so they can gamble responsibly.

Some gamblers know that such control is impossible for them. Several states offer these people another tool. California, Illinois, Indiana, Michigan, Mississippi, Missouri, and New Jersey have all passed laws allowing problem gamblers to place themselves on self-exclusion lists. By doing so, gamblers bar themselves from even entering a gambling establishment. Casinos receive a self-excluded gambler's photo and other identifying information. If the gambler tries to visit a casino and is recognized, the casino may refuse entry, wagering, check cashing, and other services.

Self-exclusion is an extreme measure, and the casinos' enforcement of the bans has come under question. Skeptics argue that casinos have little motivation to keep people out of their casinos, even when self-exclusion laws require it of them. Despite these problems, for a small number of players, self-exclusion is the only way to protect themselves from their gambling urges.

Gambler, casino sue each other

**From the Pages of
USA TODAY**

Jenny Kephart's fondness for the blackjack table took her to a world of private jet rides, her own table and dealer in casinos, and lavish hotel suites where iced champagne awaited her arrival. "My every whim," recalled Kephart, 52, a woman from suburban Nashville, who admits she was a compulsive gambler. She says she has lost more than $900,000 at casinos across the country.

Eventually, her gambling brought her to Caesars Indiana in Harrison County and put her deep in debt. Now she is at the center of a court case that tests whether a casino has a duty to protect an addicted gambler from him- or herself. The casino sued Kephart in January for failing to repay $125,000 she borrowed during a visit in March 2006 to the Harrah's-owned riverboat, a company that had been making her special offers for years.

Kephart, who is unemployed, is fighting back with a counterclaim alleging Caesars enticed her with giveaways and made money for gambling available to her, even though trained casino workers should have identified her as a problem gambler. She said casino executives knew she had come out of bankruptcy four years earlier when Harrah's was one of her creditors.

Caesars' lawyer, Stephen Langdon, argued that Kephart never asked to be banned from the casino or other Harrah's properties, so the casino had no way to know she was a problem gambler. Caesars argued that Kephart's counterclaim should be dismissed.

Kephart's lawyer, Terry Noffsinger of Evansville, says pathological gambling is widely viewed as a mental illness. He argued that Caesars representatives took "affirmative steps to persuade her to gamble" by calling her at home.

In similar cases, Indiana courts have held that casino operators don't have to prevent customers from gambling and consequently aren't responsible for their losses. Noffsinger stressed that the law is not fully settled in cases involving problem gambling.

"If she had just gone in (to Caesars) on her own, that would be one thing," Noffsinger said. He will try to prove casino officials knew Kephart was an addicted gambler and they pursued her because she had money to spare from a $1 million family inheritance she received in 2004. The casino lawyers declined to comment further.

Indiana gambling regulations allow casinos to lend money to people they deem credit-worthy. Noffsinger previously represented Evansville resident and professed gambling addict David Williams in a federal lawsuit in which the precedent that casinos have no duty to protect a compulsive gambler from himself was upheld.

California lawyer I. Nelson Rose, a gambling law expert, said he believes the court precedent is well established. He said wealthy gamblers are offered credit of several hundreds of thousands of dollars, so Caesars' decision to lend Kephart large sums is not unusual. Noffsinger said Kephart's case is different because Caesars sued her first and the casino invited her to visit.

—Grace Schneider

Above: Jenny Kephart lost much of her money playing blackjack. This card game, also known as Twenty-one, is one of the most popular casino card games worldwide.

CHAPTER THREE

Lotto Mania: State-Sponsored Gambling

O N DECEMBER 24, 2002, ANDREW "JACK" WHITTAKER was just a hardworking West Virginia family man. He had grown up with little money but had built up a successful construction company. Business was good, and Whittaker had more than enough money to keep his family comfortable for the foreseeable future. But that didn't stop Whittaker from dreaming of more. Like many Americans, he enjoyed playing the lottery in hopes of hitting a jackpot.

Everything changed on the morning of December 25. That was the day Whittaker got the news that would change his life forever. He had bought the winning ticket for Powerball, a huge multistate lottery. The jackpot: nearly $315 million.

Whittaker and his family became instant celebrities. TV and newspaper reporters wanted to know how the Whittakers would spend their new fortune. Whittaker vowed to use his winnings to help those in need.

Left: Andrew "Jack" Whittaker *(right)* and his family pose with a ceremonial check representing his Powerball winnings.

"I wanted to build churches," he said. "I wanted to get people food that didn't have food. I wanted to provide clothing for children that needed clothing."

He set about doing exactly that. He donated more than fifteen million dollars in the first few months. He established a charitable foundation to give away much of the remaining money. The pile of requests for money grew and grew. Whittaker got so many letters that the post office refused to deliver them all to his home. Many requests were from worthy causes. Others were from people asking him to pay for mundane things, such as new carpeting.

Soon people were hounding Whittaker for money everywhere he went. He could barely leave the house without being accosted. Others stole from him. People sued his construction company for flimsy reasons, hoping to squeeze some cash from its suddenly rich owner.

Whittaker was miserable. "I just got to the point that I just couldn't tolerate what was happening to me anymore," he said. "I would fly off the handle and if somebody wanted to fight me, I'd fight them. I just didn't care."

Two years later, Whittaker's granddaughter turned up dead. West Virginia state police found her wrapped in a plastic sheet behind a junked van. Officials suspect her death was drug-related. Whittaker blames the money. He says winning the lottery was a curse. He had hoped the money would change his life. It did, but not for the better.

Many lottery winners have echoed Whittaker's story. Winners often find that sudden fortune brings unexpected problems. Yet their stories don't stop millions of Americans from playing state-sponsored lotteries every year. Some people play single tickets now and then, just for fun. Others dump money they cannot truly afford into a quest to beat the astronomical odds against winning. Should federal and state governments be involved in such gambling ventures? Do the benefits produced by lottery revenues outweigh the social costs of lotteries? Americans hotly debate these questions, but they find no easy answers.

THE RETURN OF THE STATE-SPONSORED LOTTERY

State-sponsored lotteries were common in the young United States. They disappeared for about a century, from the mid-1800s to the mid-1900s. In 1963 New Hampshire resurrected the idea. The state was in desperate need of revenue, and lawmakers refused to raise taxes.

So lawmakers looked to the past and came up with a lottery, which they called a sweepstakes, to raise money. Half the proceeds would go to a state education fund. The other half would go to prizewinners.

The 1964 New Hampshire sweepstakes was a bit disappointing. It raised less than six million dollars—barely half the amount lawmakers had anticipated. And the revenue dwindled over the next several years. The decline was partly due to events in New York.

Above: New Hampshire governor John King buys the first ticket in the state's first lottery in 1964.

Many New Yorkers were participating in New Hampshire's lottery. So in 1967, New York started a lottery of its own. The state reasoned that if its citizens were going to gamble, their money might as well stay in New York. As New Yorkers began playing the lottery in their home state, fewer people played the New Hampshire sweepstakes.

The modern lottery system got off the ground in New York in 1974. Each player chose six numbers between one and thirty-six. If a player matched the six numbers randomly drawn by lottery officials, he or she won the jackpot. The odds of winning were almost two million to one. Drawings occurred weekly. If the jackpot went unclaimed, it simply rolled over into the next week's jackpot. The jackpot grew and grew, soon topping ten million dollars. Huge jackpots grabbed the public's attention. In the first year of this format, the New York lottery brought in almost two hundred million dollars. That figure more than doubled within five years.

Other states followed suit, and the state-sponsored lottery

movement was off. Soon enormous multistate lotteries such as the Powerball were raising jackpots of one hundred million dollars or more. As the stakes grew and grew, so did interest—and controversy.

LOTTO LOVE

The lottery offers a unique promise to players. A small investment provides a chance to win a huge fortune. Multimillion-dollar jackpots are irresistible to many players. Some fail to understand how small the chance of winning is. For example, the odds of a Powerball ticket winning the grand prize are 1 in 195,249,054. Others understand the odds

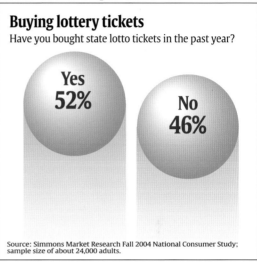

USA TODAY Snapshots®

Buying lottery tickets
Have you bought state lotto tickets in the past year?

Yes 52%

No 46%

Source: Simmons Market Research Fall 2004 National Consumer Study; sample size of about 24,000 adults.

By Shannon Reilly and Sam Ward, USA TODAY, 2005

Lottery Revenues

How do states invest revenue from gambling? Here are a few examples:

Illinois—education
Massachusetts—police and fire departments
Minnesota—environmental conservation
Pennsylvania—health care for the elderly

Above: A teacher works with children in a pre-kindergarten program in Memphis, Tennessee. The program is funded in part by proceeds from the Tennessee Lottery.

and play anyway, just for the fun of dreaming. For many, the lottery drawing is a cheap form of entertainment—nothing more.

State governments love lotteries and other forms of state-sponsored gambling too. Some form of legal wagering is available in every U.S. state except Utah and Hawaii. Gambling provides revenue that would otherwise be unavailable. This revenue often supports education, transit, and environmental protection. Many valuable programs would disappear without lottery proceeds.

Lottery revenue allows state lawmakers to help more people without raising taxes. For this reason, many see it as a valuable budget-balancing tool. With antitax sentiment growing in the United States, many lawmakers flatly refuse to raise taxes at all. That refusal creates a need for new streams of revenue. Many lawmakers see lotteries as a voluntary tax. Only those who choose to play have to pay it, minimizing political fallout for lawmakers.

According to a Gallup Poll, roughly half of adult Americans

USA TODAY Snapshots®

Midwest is most game for lottery

People in the USA who purchase state lottery tickets spend an average of $19 a month. By region:

Midwest
$27 a month

East
$21 a month

West
$13 a month

South
$13 a month

Source: Gallup Poll, December 2003

By Joseph Popiolkowski and Sam Ward, USA TODAY, 2004

buy lottery tickets. Americans spend about sixty billion dollars per year on the tickets, generating almost eighteen billion dollars in state revenues. Supporters argue that the vast majority of people favor allowing such games and that lotteries give ordinary people a chance to dream big.

But opponents believe many players don't understand that their dreams are pipe dreams. A 1999 study showed that more than half of low-income lottery players believed that winning the lottery was their best shot at getting rich. "For a lot of low-income people, the only prospect of a sudden improvement in economic circumstances is playing the lottery," said economics professor and coauthor of the study George Loewenstein.

> **"People pretend it's free money. It's not. The revenue comes from the poorest, most vulnerable, and it comes with huge social costs in addiction, bankruptcy, crime and corruption.**
>
> **—MARYLAND COMPTROLLER PETER FRANCHOT**
> USA TODAY · JANUARY 10, 2008

Playing the Odds

In most lotteries, if nobody wins the jackpot, it rolls over to the next drawing. The jackpot grows and grows until someone wins. A player can actually beat the odds (guarantee a profit) if the jackpot gets big enough. In such a case, purchasing every combination of numbers would cost less than the jackpot is worth.

In 1992 an Australian group tried to cash in on this principle. When a Virginia lottery jackpot got big enough, the group used computers to try to purchase every possible combination of numbers. Ultimately, the group ran out of time. The group had bought about 80 percent of possible combinations at drawing time. Luckily, the winning number was among them. Many other lottery players were irate about the group's actions. After this incident, the Virginia lottery outlawed the use of computers to buy massive amounts of tickets.

Most lottery tickets cost one to five dollars, though some cost thirty dollars or more. A single lottery ticket is usually a small and fairly harmless investment. Most players are content to buy a ticket or two, staying well within their means. Unfortunately, some gamblers aren't satisfied with a single ticket. Studies show that just 5 percent of players buy more than 50 percent of tickets. They may buy dozens at once, several times per week. Some players can afford that many tickets.

But often, high-volume ticket buyers are people who cannot afford it.

Opponents of legalized gambling argue that as gambling becomes more accessible, the rate of gambling addiction rises. Gambling addiction can result in lost wages, more personal bankruptcies, and even an increased crime rate.

Lotteries are not, of course, the only type of state-sponsored gambling. They're just the most prevalent. Forty-one U.S. states operate lotteries.

Some states offer other types of gambling, such as racetracks, casinos, and keno halls. (Keno is a lottery-like game in which players try to match a set of randomly drawn numbers.) In the late 1980s and early 1990s, several states legalized riverboat casinos. These floating casinos—which often provide entertainment, dining, and scenery in addition to gambling—serve the dual purpose of raising revenue and promoting tourism. Many people find riverboat casinos tolerable because they are small and have limited ability to expand. Their quaint, old-time feel also appeals to many.

Above: The *Belle of Orleans* casino riverboat docks in New Orleans, Louisiana. The custom-built boat evokes the elegant style of the United States in the early nineteenth century.

Unclaimed Riches

Some lottery winners never claim their prizes. In 2002 the owner of an Indiana Powerball ticket worth $51.7 million never spoke up. In 2007 a New York ticket worth $31 million was never cashed in. Many people discard winning scratch-off tickets for small amounts. When lottery prizes go unclaimed, the money goes back to the states.

Missed chances

States having the most unclaimed lottery prize money last year (in millions):

N.Y	**$73.6**
Texas	**$58.9**
Fla.	**$48.4**
Ohio	**$33.4**
Calif.	**$29.4**

Source: Individual state lotteries

By Julie Snider, USA TODAY, 2007

UNREALISTIC EXPECTATIONS?

A government can take one of four roles in gambling: prohibition, tolerance, regulation, or operation. For good or bad, many state governments have gravitated toward operation, or active participation in gambling. The main reason for this move is to make money.

But does the revenue generated by state-sponsored gambling meet government expectations and justify the cost of operation? Not always. For example, Ohio planned for annual revenues of nearly

> " When there's a recession and the alternatives are raising taxes or cutting services, gaming looks pretty attractive. "
>
> —**FRANK FAHRENKOPF JR.**, PRESIDENT OF THE AMERICAN GAMING ASSOCIATION AND FORMER REPUBLICAN NATIONAL COMMITTEE CHAIRMAN

USA TODAY · AUGUST 9, 2002

three hundred million dollars from a state-run keno game but took in less than fifty million dollars.

In 2007 Kansas passed a law allowing state-sponsored casinos. The state planned to build casinos on four sites, using private companies to run the facilities. Lawmakers expected to generate revenues of two hundred million dollars per year for the state. But the private companies disagreed with the state's projections. They pulled out of three of the proposed casinos, which were not built, severely curtailing the expected revenue.

Illinois lawmakers hoped to solve a state budget problem by selling a casino license to a private party. The state planned to make a lump sum of $575 million on the sale—money Illinois desperately needed. But the state's expectations were unrealistic. The state ultimately sold the license for just $125 million, not nearly enough to help balance the budget.

Above: A California lottery player shows off her tickets. The 2007 introduction of the Mega Millions game pushed California jackpots up to $500 million.

Money woes drive some states to gambling; Opponents bet that the benefits don't outweigh the costs

From the Pages of
USA TODAY

The slumping economy and dismal state finances could set off a fast-spreading wave of legalized gambling. Nineteen states are considering proposals to add video slot machines at racetracks. Twelve are studying whether to introduce or expand casino gambling, and four are debating lotteries.

"There's a new wave of expansion," says Steve Rittvo, a gambling industry consultant from New Orleans. "Gaming provides a strong revenue source, and it's almost a voluntary tax."

The debates over gambling come as states struggle by June 30 to close almost $26 billion in gaps between planned spending and tax receipts. The competition among states for gamblers' dollars is fierce. State leaders who watch bettors cross into neighboring states to buy lottery tickets or play slot machines face pressure to adopt or expand gambling.

Some states are seeking profit-sharing arrangements with Native American-owned casinos. Under the federal Indian Gaming Regulatory Act, such casinos are exempt from state taxes.

Many states see gambling as an economic development tool, Rittvo says. "The choices in an economic downturn are, do you cut services or do you increase taxes?" says Frank Fahrenkopf, president and CEO of the American Gaming Association, a trade group for commercial casinos in 11 states.

But opponents of legalized gambling warn that it's no panacea. "If this was such a good product, why didn't states automatically do this before?" says the Rev. Tom Grey, executive director of the National Coalition Against Gambling Expansion. "A lot of the states with budget deficits already have gambling. They're going to expand gambling to get more money. They're acting like gamblers."

He and other opponents of legalized gambling say gambling addiction costs the nation in lost wages, higher bankruptcy filings and increased crime. A national commission estimated in 1999 that the country has 1.8 million to 2.5 million gambling addicts.

Every state except Utah and Hawaii has some form of legalized gambling. But efforts to expand or bring gambling into a state usually meet stiff local opposition.

As states rush to embrace gambling, Martin Baird, a Phoenix consultant on ways to make it more attractive to the public, cautions: "Gaming is not the solution to poor tax planning, poor budgeting and the bad economy."

—Larry Copeland

Above: Billionaire Sheldon Adelson presents the brand-new Palazzo Las Vegas Resort Hotel Casino at its opening in 2008. The city of Las Vegas hoped to profit from business at the complex's convention center as well.

Above: In 2008 San Francisco's mass transit system, including this Bay Area Rapid Transit (BART) route, served a record number of riders. As fewer people stopped to buy gas—and lottery tickets—California saw a steep decline in the gambling proceeds used to fund public projects.

Even when states plan realistically, economic recession can blindside state gambling revenues. As the U.S. and world economies tanked in late 2008 and early 2009, many people struggled financially. They looked for ways to cut their personal spending. Lotteries and other forms of gambling were easy targets. Lottery ticket sales in several states dropped markedly.

One California official blamed the drop partly on gas prices. People used mass transit more, and they bought less gasoline. Gas stations sell a lot of lottery tickets. Fewer trips to the gas station meant fewer ticket sales. Economically speaking: when it rains, it pours—and when it's dry, it's bone dry. Just when a state really needs gambling revenue, that revenue is likely to drop sharply.

Unfair Practices?

Scratch-off lottery tickets are a hit with those seeking instant fun. But scratch-off programs present an ethical question. Many scratch-off programs have just a few big prizes—or even a single grand prize. What is a state to do when someone wins the last of the big prizes but still has tickets to sell? The promise of a big prize is the reason most players buy scratch-off tickets. Should a state discontinue the program or keep selling tickets?

Many states continue selling the tickets. These states argue that smaller prizes are still available and that their practices are stated on their websites. But most players never know that their chance of winning a big prize is zero. Lawsuits in a handful of states have forced sales to stop once the big prizes are gone.

Above: Scratch-off lottery games like these caused an uproar in South Carolina, where a player sued the state lottery for selling tickets after the big prizes had been won.

Supporters often tout state-sponsored gambling as an easy solution to budget problems. But lawmakers sometimes expect unrealistic income from gambling. If revenues don't stack up, states can face severe deficits. Programs funded by gambling—such as education and environmental protection—often take the hit.

IS IT HYPOCRITICAL?

States outlaw various forms of gambling to protect people from their own vices. But then they turn around and spearhead other forms of the outlawed activity. All forms of gambling carry the potential for addiction. If states truly want to protect problem gamblers from themselves, why do they offer gambling at all? Critics point out this hypocrisy on the part of states. Publicly, states express concern about problem gambling. But their actions don't demonstrate concern.

At the extremes of the legalized gambling debate are those who think all gambling should be outlawed and those who think all gambling should be legal. Both groups agree that states banning some forms of gambling while sponsoring others are being hypocritical. Critics argue that for these states, it's all about money. The states not only want a piece of the action, they want all the action. They're creating and enforcing a government monopoly.

> " **It might indeed be unwise to rely on gaming revenue for critical state services, but that does not mean we should leave all the money on the table.** "

—**GREG STUMBO,** SPEAKER OF THE KENTUCKY HOUSE OF REPRESENTATIVES
USA TODAY · FEBRUARY 9, 2009

Above: Maryland comptroller Peter Franchot speaks at a 2007 rally protesting a proposal to legalize slot machine gambling in the state. He argued that the state should not make money off gambling because it exploits poor people.

Lotteries and other forms of state-sponsored gambling aren't likely to go away anytime soon—nor are their critics. Despite the pitfalls, many states have become dependent on gambling revenue. Taking it away would create budgetary nightmares. States would have to cut important programs and raise taxes. So opponents often focus on preventing the further spread of gambling. Rather than try to reverse past decisions, they argue against relying on gambling revenue. But with most people supporting legalized gambling and governments needing more and more money, opponents face an uphill battle. For good or bad, U.S. state-sponsored gambling is probably here to stay.

More states roll the dice on slots

From the Pages of USA TODAY

The number of slot machines is soaring as states seek more revenue and gamblers increasingly move from table games to the flashy electronic devices. The USA had a record 767,418 slot machines and video poker games in operation on Jan. 1, up 6.4% from a year earlier, according to *Casino City Press*, an industry publication. The nation now has slots in 37 states—up from 31 in 2000—and the equivalent of one machine for every 395 residents.

The trend will accelerate in the next few years. More than 100,000 new slot machines already have regulatory approval or could get it this year. "Slots are considered an easier tax to impose" than income or sales taxes, says Alan Meister, an economist at Analysis Group in Los Angeles who studies gambling.

What's happening nationwide:

- California. Voters decide Feb. 5 whether to approve a deal to allow 17,000 new slot machines at tribal casinos. Gov. Arnold Schwarzenegger says the deal would bring the state about $400 million a year.
- Maryland. Voters in November will decide whether to allow 15,000 slot machines at racetracks, reaping the state up to $650 million a year.
- Florida. The federal government last week approved Gov. Charlie Crist's deal with the Seminole tribe to expand its seven casinos and add computerized slots. The tribe will pay the state at least $100 million a year. Separately, Miami-Dade County voters will consider slots at racetracks Jan. 29.
- Kentucky. Gov. Steve Beshear has made a statewide referendum to legalize slots a top priority.

Massachusetts and Texas legislators will consider slot machines this year. Ohio, where voters rejected slots last year, is the only large state without slots or an active push to get the machines. Indiana, Kansas, New York and Oklahoma are among states that will dramatically expand slots this year or get them for the first time.

What's driving the push for more slots: The weakening economy has slowed state revenue growth to its lowest level in five years. States get $8 billion a year in gambling taxes and fees, spending it on education, economic development and other programs. Unlike lottery proceeds—often reserved for schools—most states give legislators free rein on how gambling revenue is spent.

The success of Pennsylvania's new slot machines has attracted national attention. The state took in $580 million in slot machine revenue in 2007, its first year of gambling, and only 12,000 of the maximum 61,000 slots are operating.

Maryland Comptroller Peter Franchot will campaign against slots in November. "People pretend it's free money," he says. "It's not. The revenue comes from the poorest, most vulnerable, and it comes with huge social costs in addiction, bankruptcy, crime and corruption."

—Dennis Cauchon

Above: Gamblers play slots at the Prairie Meadows Racetrack and Casino in Altoona, Iowa. In 2009, Iowa lawmakers considered approving more casino licenses to meet increasing demand for gambling venues.

CHAPTER FOUR

Indian Gaming

CALIFORNIA GOVERNOR ARNOLD SCHWARZENEGGER got the attention of Californians—and Native Americans across the nation—in 2004. He urged voters to oppose Proposition 70, which would have extended exclusive casino gaming rights to Indian tribes for ninety-nine years. The proposed law would also have ended the limit of two thousand slot machines per casino and allowed large-scale expansion. Taxation of Native American casinos would have stayed fixed at about 8 percent—a figure Schwarzenegger considered far too low. He wanted the casinos to pay as much as 25 percent.

The state's budget was in a severe crisis. "The Indian tribes in California are not paying their fair share [in taxes]," Schwarzenegger said. His comments sparked a firestorm. Many agreed with him. But others said his comments revealed a resentment that many people felt toward Indian tribes.

"The Indians are newly rich and they're influential, all the things that can make you a target of envy," said San Diego State University sociologist Gordon Clanton.

Left: Governor Arnold Schwarzenegger raises a sign opposing the expansion of legalized gambling during a political rally in Del Mar, California, in 2004.

"Envy is not a wish for what the other person has, but the darker wish that they would lose it because you don't have it."

The incident was just one example of the passionate debate on Indian gaming playing out all over the United States. Should Native American communities have special gaming rights? What obligations do tribes have to the states in which they operate? Does gambling provide a net benefit or loss to Native Americans?

In California huge, well-funded campaigns presented both sides of the issue. Supporters of the propositions argued that gaming offered a way out of poverty for Native Americans, who had historically been one of the poorest groups in the state. They claimed the 8 percent tax rate was consistent with the rate paid by

Above: Naomi Sitting Bear watches children playing near her home on the Pine Ridge Reservation in South Dakota in 2009. Pine Ridge is the eighth-largest reservation in the United States and also one of the poorest U.S. regions.

Above: The Morongo Band of Mission Indians operates the Morongo Casino Resort and Spa in Cabazon, California.

other corporations and that a 25 percent tax rate was unfair. Opponents of the propositions echoed Schwarzenegger's comments. They said that an 8 percent tax rate, along with unchecked expansion, gave Indian tribes an unfair advantage and a monopoly on California's gambling.

Ultimately, California voters sided with their governor. About 75 percent of voters opposed the propositions. But the debate is far from over. In dozens of U.S. states, citizens continue to battle over how far tribal gaming rights extend.

THE INDIAN GAMING REGULATORY ACT

In the 1987 decision *California v. Cabazon Band of Mission Indians*, the U.S. Supreme Court gave tribal governments the authority to set up gaming operations

States with Indian Gaming

Alabama	Montana
Alaska	Nebraska
Arizona	Nevada
California	New Mexico
Colorado	New York
Connecticut	North Carolina
Florida	North Dakota
Idaho	Oklahoma
Iowa	Oregon
Kansas	South Dakota
Louisiana	Texas
Michigan	Washington
Minnesota	Wisconsin
Mississippi	Wyoming

free of state regulation. In 1988 the U.S. government passed the Indian Gaming Regulatory Act (IGRA). In broad terms, IGRA recognized the right of Native American peoples to operate casinos, bingo halls, and other gambling venues on reservation lands. (The law forced tribes to negotiate some details with individual states.) This right, not afforded to other groups in most states, gave Native Americans a virtual monopoly on gambling.

IGRA set off a national debate. Should only Native American groups have the right to operate casinos? Who should supervise them? And are these casinos a boon or a curse to the tribes who operate them?

A QUESTION OF SOVEREIGNTY

Many people question the reasoning behind IGRA. They ask why Native American peoples should have special rights. Aren't all Americans equal? Yes, but Native American nations have sovereignty, or the right to self-government, on reservations. An Indian reservation is subject to federal laws, but not to state, county, or city laws. Individual tribes have many of the same rights individual states have.

To understand Native American sovereignty, one must look back to the formation of the United States. The colonies and then the young United States dealt with Indian tribes as they dealt with foreign countries. They negotiated treaties to establish land ownership, borders, trade, and much more. The treaties were often unfair, and the United States broke many of them. But they established a nation-to-nation relationship between the tribes and the U.S. government.

As the United States matured and Native Americans integrated into U.S. society, tribal sovereignty endured. Indian tribes remain self-governing, and their sovereignty includes the right to use their lands as they see fit. How far Indian sovereignty extends is a matter of debate, however.

Above: This drawing depicts William Penn, the leader of a group of English colonists, negotiating a land purchase with members of the Delaware tribe in 1682. Like many early settlers, Penn treated Native American tribes as foreign nations.

ORDINANCE NO. 2-88
BUSINESS LICENSE REQUIRED
APPLY AT RED LAKE NATION TRIBAL GOVERNMENT CENTER

Red Lake Band of Chippewa Indians

The Red Lake Indian Nation is a Sovereign Nation.

NO PERSON IS ALLOWED TO CARRY A CONCEALED HANDGUN EXCEPT BY PERMIT OF RED LAKE LAW ENFORCEMENT.

(Pursuant to Red Lake Tribal Council Resolution 147 - 03)

Red Lake Band of Chippewa Indians

Above: A sign at the border of the Red Lake Indian Reservation in northern Minnesota reminds visitors of the Chippewa band's status as an independent nation.

Indian gaming is at the forefront of that debate. But the passage of IGRA affected more than just gaming rights. By allowing tribes to exert their sovereignty on this issue, lawmakers set a precedent (legal basis) for self-government in other areas, including taxation, education, and law enforcement. To the Native American community, gaming rights represent more than just revenue. They constantly remind people that Indian tribes are nations within a nation.

OVERSIGHT

Indian gaming rights vary widely by state. Tribes operate under different rules and pay different taxes to the states.

The Indian Gaming Regulatory Act set up the National Indian Gaming Commission (NIGC) to oversee Indian gaming. The president of the United States appoints the head of NIGC. But NIGC has relatively little power in regulating and auditing Indian casinos.

Corruption has long been a part of the gambling world, and Indian gaming is no exception. Many tribes don't really operate their own gaming facilities. Instead, they hire professionals to do so and then rely on the professionals to accurately report and distribute profits. When the "pros" behave unprofessionally, things can get ugly. Proponents of Indian gaming insist that such corruption is the exception, not the rule. Anytime you combine people with huge amounts of money, some sneaky dealings are inevitable. They say that corruption exists in any large-scale, highly profitable venture and is in no way unique to Indian gaming.

Above: A mother of the Kickapoo tribe leads her daughter through a poverty-stricken Kickapoo village in Texas in 1980.

POSITIVE IMPACT

In the middle to late 1980s, many Native American peoples were languishing in poverty. IGRA promised a badly needed economic boost. After IGRA passed, Indian casinos sprang up all around the United States. They provided jobs, as well as profits, to many. According to the National Indian Gaming Association (NIGA), by 2005 Indian gaming was providing more than twenty-two billion dollars of annual profits to tribes in twenty-eight states.

> " The jobs [provided by Indian gaming] give people the chance to pull themselves up by their bootstraps and get out of poverty. That carries over into less juvenile crime, less domestic violence and an overall better living experience for the families. "
>
> —JAMES SANDERS, DIRECTOR OF AN ADOLESCENT DRUG AND ALCOHOL TREATMENT CENTER ON THE CHEROKEE INDIAN RESERVATION IN NORTH CAROLINA, 2003

It was also responsible for about six hundred thousand jobs, many of them for non-Indians. In many states, Indian gaming has also filled government treasuries with tax revenues.

Indian gaming has vastly improved many Native American communities. Gaming leaders point out benefits that extend far beyond the bottom line. Decades ago, young people found little reason to stay on the reservation when they grew up. Few good jobs were available. A sense of community pride was lacking.

But gaming changed all that. Suddenly the reservations were thriving. Casinos and related businesses offered well-paying jobs.

Above: The popularity of the Silver Star Resort and Casino in Choctaw, Mississippi, allowed the Mississippi Band of Choctaw Indians to open three hotels, another casino, a golf club, and a water park in the area.

Reservations With Tribal Gaming

Unemployment cut by 50%

Welfare down 68%

Casinos generate $120 million in taxes each year

Above: Each year supporters and opponents of expanding legalized gambling run hundreds of commercials explaining their views. This pro-gambling ad appeared in California in 1998.

Residents began thinking differently about their communities. Carl Walking Eagle, vice chairman and gaming commissioner at Spirit Lake, North Dakota, described the impact of gaming on his community. He said tribal members gained "a new sense of pride, renewed energies and hope, that extends a sense of satisfaction to our elders, and instills purpose and dedication in our young people."

For centuries, many people of Native American descent hid their heritage. But since the passage of IGRA, more and more people have identified themselves as Native Americans. This change is due partly to a general decline in racial prejudice and a general increase in ethnic pride. Financial motivation may be another cause. Many tribes divide gaming profits among their members. So claiming a tribal heritage can be a financial boon.

NEGATIVE IMPACT

Not everyone lauds gaming as a boon to the Native American community. "I almost hate to say it, but I think there may be some people who see the casinos and the

> " The so-called Indian casinos are a joke. Their management is often about as Indian as I am. "
>
> **—ANDY ROONEY,** *60 MINUTES* COMMENTATOR, 1997

windfall profits and think there may be something for them in identifying [themselves as Native Americans]," said Bill Wells, an Indian Affairs commissioner in Tennessee.

This financial motivation has led to more scrutiny of tribal heritage claims. For the most part, tribes themselves decide who qualifies as a member. But this power can create problems. Leaders may be tempted to cast out those who oppose tribal actions and strip away their legal heritage.

Above: In 2004 the Pechanga Band of Luiseño Indians disenrolled Sophia and Lawrence Madariaga *(center)*, along with nearly one hundred others. Disenrollment strips people of their status as Native Americans, along with benefits such as health insurance and scholarships. The Madariagas pointed to greed over casino revenues as one reason for their disenrollment.

Payout or pride, more claim Indian heritage

From the Pages of USA TODAY

More Americans are identifying themselves as Native American, pushing the growth rate of that group higher than that of the USA. Those identifying themselves as at least part American Indian grew from 4.1 million in 2000 to 4.5 million last year, according to U.S. Census data released in August—a 10% increase. The total American population grew an estimated 7.7% over that period, the data show.

Demographers say the growth, too large to attribute to birth rates, comes after more than a century of Native Americans choosing to hide their ethnicity over fear of discrimination. "There's less of a stigma with Indians identifying themselves than there was in the past," says Jacqueline Johnson Pata, executive director of the National Congress of American Indians in Washington, D.C.

Some claiming Native American heritage may be motivated by finances, says Bill Wells, an Indian Affairs commissioner in Tennessee. Tribes recognized by the federal government that operate casinos take in more than $20 billion a year, according to the National Indian Gaming Commission, and sometimes pay out significant dividends to their citizens, Wells says.

"I almost hate to say it, but I think there may be some people who see the casinos and the windfall profits and think there may be something for them in identifying," Wells says.

Melba Checote-Eads of Tennessee, a citizen of the Muscogee (Creek) Nation, says she, her children and grandchildren claim their heritage. "My daddy always would say, 'Why would anyone want to be Indian?'" she says. "Today, a lot of people are doing research, they're able to find out a lot more about their families. And I think it's wonderful that some of them want to claim their heritage."

Cindy Yahola, also of Tennessee and a member of the Muscogee Nation, says she thinks some believe "if they identify themselves as Indian, they are entitled to something" like government money or preference for scholarships. Still, Yahola says she thinks "it can help us share the culture."

—Janell Ross and Clay Carey

Gaming brings other temptations too. For decades many Indian tribes have struggled with widespread drug and alcohol addiction. Some argue that gambling aggravates the problem of addiction among Native Americans.

In addition, gaming doesn't turn a profit for every tribe. Those fortunate enough to live near major metropolitan areas can benefit greatly. For example, the Shakopee Mdewakanton Sioux Community lies on the edge of Minnesota's Minneapolis–Saint Paul metropolitan area. Members of the tribe earn hundreds of thousands of dollars each year in revenue from Mystic Lake Casino, which attracts many gamblers from the city.

But tribes in more isolated areas are not so lucky. The Hualapai tribe in Arizona opened a casino in the 1990s. But the casino, which was near the Grand Canyon, attracted few visitors. Perhaps visitors were more interested in the natural beauty of the Grand Canyon, or maybe the casino

Above: An antigambling protester pickets a proposed New York casino in 2006.

Above: After the failure of a tribe-owned casino, the Hualapai turned to tourism as a source of income. In 2007 they opened the Skywalk, a glass-floored scenic path extending over the edge of the Grand Canyon, on the reservation.

was just too close to Las Vegas. Whatever the reason, the casino closed after just a year. The Hualapai had hoped the casino would be an economic boon, but instead, its failure left the tribe more than one million dollars in debt.

CHAPTER FIVE

The Pitfalls of Sports Gambling

"SHOELESS" JOE JACKSON WAS A NATURAL ON THE baseball field. The smooth-fielding, sweet-swinging outfielder seemed destined for greatness. But everything changed for Jackson in 1919.

Jackson played for the Chicago White Sox. The 1919 White Sox were a powerful team. They advanced to the World Series, where they faced the Cincinnati Reds. At the time, gambling on sporting events was very popular. The White Sox were heavy favorites, meaning most bettors expected them to win the series.

Chicago first baseman Arnold "Chick" Gandil had other ideas, however. Gandil had ties to professional gamblers. He helped hatch a plot in which he and some of his teammates would intentionally lose the World Series. Their loss would allow Gandil's associates to place heavy bets on the Reds and collect massive winnings, some of which would then go to the players.

Left: "Shoeless" Joe Jackson wears a catcher's mitt at a 1919 Chicago White Sox game. His nickname came from his having played an early game without wearing shoes.

Above: Judge Kenesaw Mountain Landis *(rear left)* questions members of the Chicago White Sox during the investigation of the 1919 Black Sox scandal. Arnold "Chick" Gandil *(rear, third from left)* was one of the players accused of cheating.

The Reds won. Rumors swirled about the White Sox throwing the series. Almost a year later, Jackson and a teammate confessed that some players on the team had lost on purpose. Major League Baseball (MLB) banned eight White Sox players, including Gandil and Jackson, from the sport for life. The team became known as the Black Sox.

Many praised MLB for its decisive action. But that action was not without controversy. Jackson, for example, insisted that he had not taken part in throwing the series. The statistics seemed to back him up. He had a .375 batting average during the series—the highest among all the players. But MLB stood firm. Jackson's career was over. Almost a century later, the debate over Shoeless Joe rages on.

The Black Sox scandal illustrates the unique problem associated with sports gambling. When gamblers bet on sporting events, cheating is more likely to occur in those events. Gamblers or bookies can work with athletes, coaches, or officials to fix the outcomes of competitions.

Gambling controversy has touched every major sport. Every time another story surfaces about a sports figure involved in gambling, people question the integrity of that sport. That's why most major sports don't tolerate sports betting of any kind among their players, coaches, or officials. The temptation to make big bucks by altering an event's outcome is just too strong for some people to resist.

SPORTS AND GAMBLING

Sports and gambling—to many people, they go together like peanut butter and jelly. As long as sports competitions have been around, people have been wagering on their outcomes. From boxing to football to horse racing, every sport has its bettors. Many gamblers consider every level of sports—professional, college, and even high school—fair game. People can bet on sports in many different ways. They can join friendly office pools on men's college basketball tournaments or patronize seedy, back-alley bookies.

Above: A bookmaker seeks bettors at a power lawnmower derby in Pennsylvania around 1955.

In the early 1990s, federal lawmakers addressed the high risk of game fixing by restricting legal sports betting. The Professional and Amateur Sports Protection Act (PASPA) of 1992 outlawed sports betting in every state except Nevada, Oregon, Montana, and Delaware. In these four places, state lawmakers decide whether to legalize sports gambling. Of the excepted states, only Nevada has legalized sports betting. (In 2009 Delaware lawmakers considered legalizing sports gambling as well.) This ban covers almost all team and individual sports, at all levels of competition. So some bettors go to the excepted states to place their bets. PASPA allows some exceptions, such as betting on the ball game of jai alai in Florida. Animal racing is another exception in all states.

Sports betting does not come without a cost to the states, however. Nevada has no franchises in any of the four major U.S. professional sports leagues covering baseball, basketball, football, and hockey. All four leagues have avoided basing teams in Las Vegas for fear that gambling could taint the game. In addition, the National Collegiate Athletic Association (NCAA) will not allow any of its basketball

Above: Jai alai is a team sport played with a ball and basketlike catching mitts. The government of Florida has created gambling laws to protect betting on jai alai games.

tournament games to be hosted in a state where legal sports betting can take place.

Despite PASPA, illegal sports wagering is rampant. Much illegal sports gambling happens each spring with March Madness, the NCAA men's basketball tournament. For many, joining a betting pool at work is key to the fun of following the games. Each player predicts how the tournament will play out. Entry fees are usually just a few dollars, but sometimes they cost much more. Because many pools are large, winners can earn substantial sums of money.

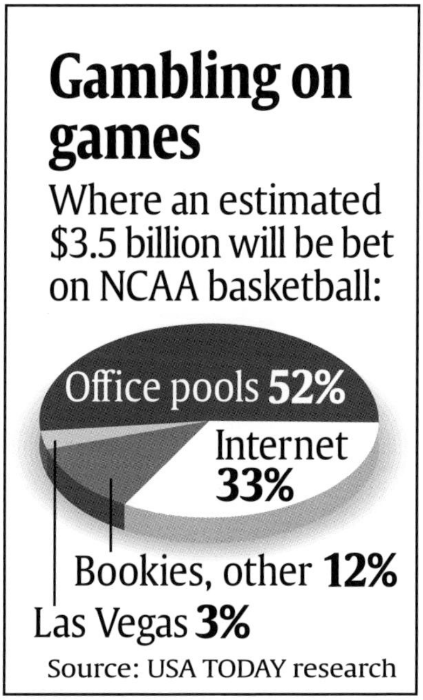

Gambling on games

Where an estimated $3.5 billion will be bet on NCAA basketball:

Office pools **52%**

Internet **33%**

Bookies, other **12%**

Las Vegas **3%**

Source: USA TODAY research

By Joni Alexander, USA TODAY, 2008

" To allow [sports] betting in Nevada and three other states is discrimination against the rest of the states. We have to do something [to change the law]. If you go to Atlantic City on Super Bowl weekend there won't be anyone there. "

—**RAY LESNIAK,** NEW JERSEY STATE SENATOR, 2009

Some gambling opponents caution that workplace betting reduces productivity at work. And since such gambling is illegal in most states, workplace betting poses legal risks to employers, who may seem to support or condone the activity. Big wins can trigger addictive behavior in some people. But to most people, these arguments ring hollow. NCAA pools are all about fun, supporters say. Predicting and betting makes the games more exciting to watch. And winning the office pool is often more about bragging rights than about money.

SPORTS BETTING SCANDALS

The Black Sox scandal is the most famous example of gambling corrupting a sporting event, but it is far from the only one. Wagering can endanger the integrity of any sport. History has given us many examples of such corruption.

In 1951 scandal rocked college basketball. Thirty-five players were accused of point-shaving (intentionally reducing the margin of victory) over a period of four years. The scandal centered on (but was not limited to) the nation's most powerful basketball

Above: A Chicago judge confronts two University of Kentucky players *(fourth and fifth from right)* with an accusation of point-shaving in a 1949 game in Chicago.

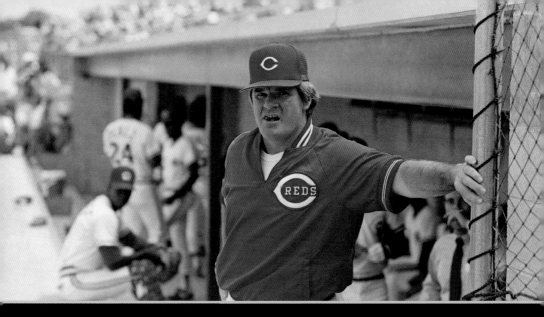

Above: Cincinnati Reds manager Pete Rose watches a game in Florida in 1989. Later that year, MLB banned him from baseball for unethical betting.

program, the University of Kentucky. The accused players included Sherman White, who had moved on to the National Basketball Association (NBA) by 1951. The NBA banned White, considered one of the finest young players in the game. His career was ruined. He was not alone. The NCAA gave the entire Kentucky basketball program the "death sentence." Kentucky could not even field a team in the 1952–1953 season.

Pete Rose was a baseball icon in the 1970s and 1980s. He became the Cincinnati Reds manager in 1984. MLB's all-time leader in hits had a dark secret, however. He was a gambling addict. A league investigation found that Rose had bet on baseball. Worse still, the investigation revealed that Rose had bet on his own team. This discovery raised questions about whether his gambling impacted the decisions he made during the game and called the integrity of Reds games into question. MLB banned him from the game in 1989. The ban cost Rose a managing career and a sure place in the National Baseball Hall of Fame.

Point-shaving remains a concern in college athletics; Gamblers seek ways to lure players into game-fixing fold

From the Pages of USA TODAY

When gambler Ghazi "Gary" Manni allegedly bribed University of Toledo running back Harvey "Scooter" McDougle Jr. and other players to rig football and basketball games from 2003 to 2006, he didn't ask them to deliberately lose, according to federal law authorities. The alleged game-fixer's pitch to McDougle was more insidious—and psychologically effective: Play to win, just by fewer points than the betting line set by the oddsmakers of Las Vegas. Don't beat yourself, beat the spread.

This illegal scam is known as point-shaving. The most common form involves paying athletes on favored teams to win the game—but by fewer points than the betting line.

If the Toledo Rockets football team were favored by 10, Manni would ask players to try to win by nine or fewer, according to an affidavit [sworn statement] in the case filed by FBI special agent Brian Max. Manni allegedly would then bet big money on the opponent to "cover the spread." And clean up.

"Is it a huge problem? I wouldn't say that. But it's a continual problem," says Matt Heron, chief of the organized crime section at FBI headquarters in Washington. "It's out there. We know it's out there. Whether we can prove it is a different matter."

Shaving points might seem like a no-harm, no-foul way to make easy money, Heron says. But a college athlete [who does it] risks his education, future career, even freedom.

Point-shaving is a federal crime. Any player caught shaving points permanently loses NCAA eligibility in all sports and can be arrested and prosecuted.

Just ask Stevin "Hedake" Smith, an ex-team captain of Arizona State who served nearly a year in prison in 1999–2000. He played briefly with the Dallas Mavericks early in 1997, but his NBA prospects disappeared after he pleaded guilty in late 1997 to conspiracy to commit sports bribery for shaving points in four games in 1994.

A less common form of point-shaving involves paying players on underdog teams to deliberately lose by more than the point spread. If the Rockets were predicted to lose by two points, Manni would tell players to lose by three or more, according to the FBI affidavit.

Even the greediest college athletes are highly competitive, experts say. It's much easier for game fixers to sell them on shaving points while still winning than losing on purpose. "If the spread is 12 points, he doesn't care if he wins by 10 or 14," says Justin Wolfers, assistant professor of business and public policy at the University of Pennsylvania's Wharton School. After studying 44,120 NCAA Division I men's basketball games from 1989 to 2005, he concluded in a research paper last year that 1%, or nearly 500 games, involved "gambling-related corruption."

Mark Andrews, chairman of the watchdog Casino Watch in Chesterfield, Mo., a suburb of St. Louis, says growing acceptance of wagering, from sports betting to poker, has created the first generation "to grow up thinking gambling is acceptable. Combine that with being in a position of influence, and they will get into trouble real quick."

Scandals involving dumping games have been scarce recently. Recall the eight Chicago White Sox players pocketing bribes to dump the 1919 World Series to the Cincinnati Reds. Or pro boxers taking dives in the ring.

During the 2006 NCAA Division I men's basketball tournament, a trainer from one of the teams making the Sweet 16 received a suspicious text-mail message asking for inside information. He reported it to the FBI.

Why a trainer? "He knows who's hurt, who's healthy, who's got a bum knee," Heron says. The only way to eradicate point-shaving, Wolfers says, would be to eliminate point-spread betting on college sports.

The dirty secret of college sports is how easy it is for fixers to bribe student-athletes who have little or no money, Hill says, especially if the players don't think they have the size or skill to make it in the professional ranks after college. "Everybody has a number. Everybody is corruptible. I don't care who it is," says Hill. "It's just a matter of how much—and how much they think they can get away with. "You offer a kid 10 large ($10,000), he's at least going to think about it."

—Michael McCarthy

Corruption isn't limited to athletes. In July 2007, reports claimed that NBA referee Tim Donaghy had been betting tens of thousands of dollars on NBA games. The reports said that Donaghy had teamed up with members of organized crime to gamble on games he officiated. His position as a referee allowed him to affect a game, especially in determining how many combined points the teams would score. Gamblers often bet on the total number of points scored in a game—a bet called the over/under.

Above: NBA referee Tim Donaghy *(lower left)* watches a 2007 game between the Washington Wizards and the Atlanta Hawks.

Statistical analysis later revealed that the teams in games officiated by Donaghy scored more points than expected by Las Vegas sportsbooks (sports betting houses) more than 57 percent of the time. Scoring more points than predicted by sportsbooks would happen 0.001 percent of the time under normal circumstances. Further, records showed that on ten games officiated by Donaghy, betting surged suspiciously just before tip-off. Donaghy pleaded guilty to gambling charges. However, he insisted that NBA games were frequently fixed and that the NBA office itself was sometimes involved.

Above: Gamblers at Bally's Race & Sports Book in Las Vegas, Nevada, can watch and bet on several sports games and horse races simultaneously.

The danger of gambling-tainted sports competitions is higher than ever, thanks to the ease and anonymity of Internet betting. Huge online sportsbooks offer wagers on almost any game, professional or amateur. (Major sports such as football, baseball, basketball, golf, and auto racing attract the most wagers by far.) Some sportsbooks reportedly have even offered wagers on the Little League World Series—a contest that features children as young as twelve years old. A college athlete could easily open an account with an Internet sportsbook and place bets on his or her own game. Few online sportsbooks have the oversight needed to catch such an incident. Even if a sportsbook could match a player's name to an account, a player could simply bet through a friend's or family member's account.

DO THE LAWS GO TOO FAR?

Most people would agree that fixing games is wrong. But does the risk of game fixing justify banning sports betting in general?

Many gamblers insist that even a small bet on a sporting event makes it more exciting to watch. They're not trying to influence the outcome of a game. They're just trying to use their knowledge to pick a winner and give themselves a rooting interest. Of course, some sports gamblers become compulsive. But that's true of any type of gambling. Should those who can control their betting be denied a legal way to pursue their hobby because others lack such self-control?

Other supporters of sports gambling argue that restrictions against athletes and coaches go too far. Critics point to the case of University of Washington football coach Rick Neuheisel. The university fired Neuheisel in the summer of 2003 after news surfaced that he had bet in an NCAA basketball pool. Neuheisel first denied the reports but later admitted to the betting. No evidence showed he'd ever bet on his own team or even on football. Neuheisel later sued the university for wrongful termination (firing) and won a $4.5 million settlement.

Where should the law draw the line? Should it ban athletes, coaches, and officials from all

> **"You'd be shocked at how many kids are [betting on sports online]. The number one form of problem gambling for college students is Internet betting on sports."**
>
> —ED LOONEY, DIRECTOR OF THE COUNCIL ON COMPULSIVE GAMBLING OF NEW JERSEY
>
> USA TODAY · AUGUST 22, 2003

> **" Without betting, there wouldn't be an NFL. People would be taking their children for walks in the park rather than being couch potatoes on Sundays. "**
>
> **—LAS VEGAS MAYOR OSCAR GOODMAN**
> **USA TODAY · NOVEMBER 30, 2005**

Above: University of Washington football coach Rick Neuheisel speaks to reporters in 2003 while suspended from coaching for gambling on NCAA basketball games.

forms of sports gambling? Or should they have the same rights as everyone else, so long as they don't bet on their own sport? Or are the problems associated with sports gambling so prevalent that only a total ban can solve them? What's more important: protecting the integrity of sports or protecting the rights of people to spend their money as they please?

CHAPTER SIX

Games of Skill

CHRIS MONEYMAKER WASN'T SUPPOSED TO BE A factor at the 2003 World Series of Poker Main Event in Las Vegas. Moneymaker was not a seasoned poker player. He was an accountant who loved to play cards. He had not put up the ten-thousand-dollar entry fee that many of the 839 entrants had paid. Instead, he had earned his seat by winning a tournament online for just forty dollars.

Amazingly, Moneymaker worked his way to the final table. There he faced some of the best poker players in the world. Former champion Dan Harrington, Vegas pro Sammy Farha, and others sat shoulder to shoulder with Moneymaker, battling for the title of world champion. First prize: $2.5 million.

The field of players dwindled, leaving just Moneymaker and Farha. That was when Moneymaker made the play that everyone would remember. With a very weak hand, he pushed all his chips into the

Left: Chris Moneymaker plays the final hand of the World Series of Poker Main Event in Las Vegas in 2003.

center of the table. This huge bluff suggested he had a very strong hand. Farha, known for his ability to read his opponent, withered under the pressure. He folded (conceded defeat on that hand), giving Moneymaker a huge chip advantage. Moneymaker soon finished off Farha. The poker world was shocked. Moneymaker, an unknown amateur, had beaten the best players to win the biggest prize in poker.

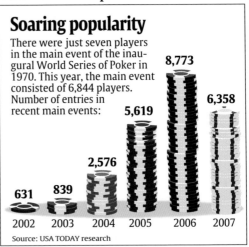

USA TODAY Snapshots®

Soaring popularity

There were just seven players in the main event of the inaugural World Series of Poker in 1970. This year, the main event consisted of 6,844 players. Number of entries in recent main events:

2002	2003	2004	2005	2006	2007
631	839	2,576	5,619	8,773	6,358

Source: USA TODAY research

By Matt Eppers and Julie Snider, USA TODAY, 2008

The game would never be the same. For decades professionals had dominated high-level poker. Moneymaker's victory inspired millions of people to take up the game. Some became winners and even superstars. Many lost a little money in exchange for their

> ❝ [Chris] Moneymaker caught a lot of people's attention. . . . I can't dunk a basketball; I'm just not big enough. I can't beat Tiger Woods in golf. But in poker . . . you can beat the best players in the world. ❞
>
> —LYLE BERMAN, POKER PROFESSIONAL
> ⓢ USA TODAY · JULY 27, 2006

Above: Professional poker player Annie Duke competes in a World Series of Poker event in 2009. Duke is one of a handful of players who has achieved celebrity status as a result of poker.

entertainment. Others lost a lot more. College students dropped out of school to play poker full-time. People quit their jobs and moved to Las Vegas to seek their fortunes. Others turned to the Internet, playing poker for hours at a time.

SKILL AND CHANCE: WHAT'S THE DIFFERENCE?

In a lottery, one person's chance of winning is as good as anyone else's. Poker has an element of chance too. But unlike a lottery, poker also requires knowledge and skill.

That's an important distinction, many argue. They say that gambling laws should apply only to games of chance. They say that gambling is, by definition, wagering on an outcome determined by chance. In a skill game, players rely on their skills and knowledge, not on chance.

> " **Gambling is a part of life, at the card table or in business. That said, poker is a stupid way to make a living. The correct way for a kid to be taught poker is to learn that it is a very difficult game with a high degree of risk.** "
>
> —**BARRY SCHULMAN,** PUBLISHER OF *CARD PLAYER* MAGAZINE
> **USA TODAY · DECEMBER 21, 2004**

Many people compare playing games of skill to investing in the stock market. A stock investor uses knowledge to guide buying and selling decisions, and those decisions determine how much money he or she makes or loses. Games of skill work much the same way.

A stock investment can make or lose money, but nobody classifies it as gambling. Many contend that the law should treat skill games the same way it treats stock investments. But in many U.S. states, the law treats chance games and skill games the same way.

Poker is just one example of a skill game often played for money. Another is backgammon, a board game that's very popular in

Above: The royal flush is the highest-ranking poker hand. Although cards come randomly, players must use their skill in evaluating their hand's relative strength.

Above: Students at a school in Atlanta, Georgia, learn to play chess. The class uses the game to demonstrate that players must depend on skill, not luck, in their decision making.

Middle Eastern countries. Both games blend skill and chance. A skillful player has an advantage over an unskilled player, but with enough luck, even an unskilled player can come out on top in the short term.

Other games are entirely skill-based. Chess, for example, contains no element of luck. A player can rely only on his or her wits to win.

How should gambling laws apply to games of skill? Should all forms of gambling follow the same rules, or should games of skill be treated differently? If the latter, what about games like blackjack, which are mostly chance with a very small element of skill?

GAME OF SKILL OR CHANCE?	
GAME	**TYPE**
Roulette	Chance
Lottery	Chance
Dice games	Chance
Poker	Skill and chance
Backgammon	Skill and chance
Blackjack	Skill and chance
Chess	Skill
Checkers	Skill

Fantasy Sports

In fantasy sports, "owners" draft and operate virtual teams of players from a sports league such as the NFL or MLB. Owners use player stats to score points, competing for the high score in an imaginary game or in a given time period. Owners in a league compete with one another over the course of a season, with the winner taking the league title. Betting leagues are common. Each owner pays into a prize pool, and winners can take home big money.

Are fantasy sports games of chance or skill? Owners must use their knowledge of the sport to make smart decisions. But the same is true of sports betting, which the law does not view as a game of skill.

Bettors have no control over the outcomes of sports competitions, whether those competitions are real or imaginary. But curiously, fantasy sports are considered games of skill. Therefore, cash fantasy leagues are legal in most states that allow wagering on games of skill.

LEGAL STATUS

The regulatory debate over gambling on games of skill versus games of chance has gone on for decades. The legal status of poker and similar games is in question. Pennsylvania is one of the biggest and most publicized battlegrounds for the issue.

In 2007 Pennsylvania officials charged attorney Larry Burns with running an illegal gambling venture. Burns had organized poker tournaments at a local fire hall and had profited from them. Authorities confiscated more than ten thousand dollars of his earnings. Burns fought the charges, saying that since poker was a game of skill and not a game of chance, the tournaments were not an instance of gambling and therefore were not illegal.

District Attorney John Peck disagreed. "Whether you win or lose, [a poker outcome is] based essentially in the cards you are dealt and that's

> " **Successful [poker] players must possess intellectual and psychological skills. They must know the rules and the mathematical odds. They must know how to read their opponents' 'tells' and styles. They must know when to hold and fold and raise. They must know how to manage their money.** "

—PENNSYLVANIA JUDGE THOMAS JAMES IN HIS RULING THAT POKER IS A GAME OF SKILL, NOT CHANCE, 2009

Above: Friends enjoy a game of poker at home.

by chance. It meets the definition of gambling." The judge agreed with Peck, ruling that poker was a game based on chance. Therefore, betting on poker was an illegal form of gambling in Pennsylvania.

The question resurfaced in Pennsylvania in 2009. The case involved a Pennsylvania couple that held low-stakes Texas Hold'em games (a form of poker) in their home. The couple did not charge a rake (a percentage of bets taken for profit). Even so, authorities arrested

A Friend in the White House

U.S. poker players got a boost with the 2008 election of President Barack Obama. Obama had mentioned in several interviews during his campaign that he was a poker fan. He watched poker tournaments on TV and liked to play the game as well. He reportedly carried a poker chip with him as a good luck charm.

Big-name poker stars Phil Ivey and Daniel Negreanu threw their support behind Obama. The two stars attended a campaign rally, where Obama spotted and recognized them. According to Negreanu, Obama excitedly pulled out sixty dollars and told the pair how he'd won the money the previous night in a poker game with his staff. Because of the president's passion for poker, many players hope that he will support legislation recognizing poker as a game of skill.

Above: World Series of Poker champion Phil Ivey started competing in poker tournaments as a teenager.

the couple after an undercover Pennsylvania state trooper took part in one of their games. Officials charged the couple with more than twenty counts of illegal gambling. The Poker Players Alliance (PPA) sprang to the couple's defense.

Judge Thomas James presided over the case. James applied what he called a "dominant factor" test to the case. "Simply, if chance

Above: Members of the Poker Players Alliance take part in a 2009 briefing in Washington, D.C. Legislators sought their ideas on the regulation of Internet poker games.

predominates, Texas Hold'em is gambling," James said. "If skill predominates, it is not gambling. . . . It is apparent that skill predominates over chance in Texas Hold'em poker." James ruled that the couple's Texas Hold'em games were not gambling and therefore not illegal. The couple was cleared of charges. PPA declared the decision a major victory. PPA officials said that the case set an important precedent—especially for online poker. New laws were under consideration to ban online gambling. Making a distinction between games of skill and games of chance would be important to the discussion.

CHAPTER SEVEN

Bingo! Charitable Gambling

AS STATES RELY ON GAMBLING FOR REVENUE, SO DO many charities and nonprofit organizations. Every state except Utah and Hawaii has laws legalizing some form of charitable gambling, with regulations spelling out how much can be wagered, what it can be bet on, how prizes should be distributed, and more.

Charities depend on a variety of games to make money. Some hold special "Las Vegas nights," "Monte Carlo nights," or "millionaire parties" that feature traditional casino table games such as blackjack. Many charities hold raffles, selling tickets for a chance to win a prize. Others rely on pull tabs, multilayered paper tickets containing symbols hidden behind perforated tabs. Like scratch-off lottery tickets, pull tabs provide instant play and instant winnings. Charity Texas Hold'em poker nights are also increasingly popular. But all of those games pale in importance to the king of charitable gambling: bingo.

Left: A bingo player plays several cards at once during a game hosted by the Perdix Fire Company station in Perdix, Pennsylvania. The volunteer fire department depends on the games to raise most of its money.

Above: A family plays bingo, using beans as counters, at a carnival gaming hall in New York City in about 1940.

THE BINGO REVOLUTION

Bingo got its start at 1920s carnivals. Players arranged a set of cards, each with a number, in rows. Then players placed beans on the numbers as they were called out by a carnival pitchman. When a player had covered a full row of numbers with beans, he or she shouted "beano" and collected a prize.

Edwin Lowe, a New York toy salesman, witnessed the game at a Florida carnival in 1929. He was amazed at the game's ability to captivate crowds. The beano area was so busy that Lowe couldn't even get a seat to play. The game continued on into the early morning.

Seeing a business opportunity, Lowe made his own beano set and brought it back to New York with him. The game proved just as popular there. Lowe had a hit on his hands. One night a woman, excited at having filled a row with beans, mistakenly called out, "Bingo!" Lowe liked the ring of that word. He began

Bingo's Origins

Historians believe bingo evolved from an Italian game called Lo Giuoco del Lotto d'Italia. Italians still play this game, which is run by the government of Italy. It contributes millions of dollars in revenue to the Italian government.

producing the game under the name *bingo*.

It wasn't long before shouts of "Bingo!" were ringing through community centers, church basements, and dedicated bingo halls across the nation and around the world. By 1934 the United States held an estimated ten thousand bingo games per week. The game has evolved since Lowe's first version. The modern system appeared in the mid-1930s. By 1974 thirty-five states had legalized the game for fundraising purposes. By the early twenty-first century, that number had climbed to forty-eight. Even in states where bingo remains illegal, law enforcement often looks the other way.

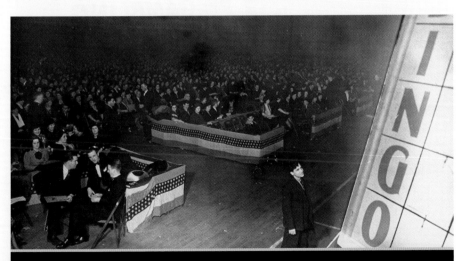

Above: Thousands play bingo at a fund-raiser for a Catholic church in Jersey City, New Jersey, in 1938.

> " **There's a moral question about using gambling to support a program for children. . . . [But] we need the $350,000 that gambling brings us every year.** "

—**DON HALL,** BOYS AND GIRLS CLUBS OF KING COUNTY, WASHINGTON, 1993

APPROPRIATE FOR CHARITY?

But while many people and organizations embrace charitable gambling, others cry foul. Charitable gambling is especially troubling to many churchgoers. Church leaders often preach that gambling is a sin and a display of greed. It is not the sort of behavior a good, God-fearing person takes part in. Meanwhile, many churches rely on bingo nights and other gambling events as fund-raisers.

How do churchgoers reconcile the conflicting messages? Many people reason that gambling is not a sin when it is done for the

Above: Clergy and members of the United Methodist Church protest the expansion of gambling in Bethlehem, Pennsylvania, in 2009.

Above: Senior citizens play bingo in the basement of Saint Patrick's Church in Watertown, Massachusetts, in 2007. The expansion of casino and online gambling threatened not only the church's fund-raising efforts but also the social time enjoyed by regular players.

greater good. Others argue that such a distinction is illogical. If gambling is wrong, it is always wrong. If a church or charitable organization reaps the profits, that doesn't change the moral issues attached to gambling.

Another argument against charitable gaming—bingo in particular—is that it appeals to the poorest segments of society. Opponents of charitable gambling argue that preying upon the poor is wrong. Others see the game simply as cheap entertainment. A night of bingo costs little more than going to a movie, and bingo players have the chance to walk away as winners.

A BLURRED LINE

The landscape of gambling in the United States has changed a lot since bingo gained popularity in the 1930s. Casinos have sprung up all over. States are sponsoring more and more lotteries, including instant scratch-off games and video lottery. Online gaming has changed the way people see gambling and has made access easier than ever.

Charity bingo trying 'to reinvent itself'

From the Pages of
USA TODAY

Julia Eddy has volunteered at bingo games for more than 20 years. She remembers the glory days. "It used to be 180 to 200 (people) whenever you opened the doors," says Eddy, 39, who manages three charity bingo games a week in Aurora, Colo., near Denver.

Now on a Saturday morning, fewer than half that number show up. Several bingo halls in the area have closed in the past year for lack of business, she says.

Charities that run bingo games for money to sponsor food pantries, recreation programs for poor children and other activities are scrambling to find new customers. That's because many players are flocking to casinos instead, drawn by bigger jackpots and flashier surroundings.

To help charities compete, gaming regulators are enabling non-profit groups to increase jackpots and use electronic gadgets that make it easier for customers to play several bingo cards at once. They're also requiring bingo hall owners to spruce up their venues to make them more fun for players.

"You can't make much with bake sales and car washes," says Corky Kyle, executive director of the Colorado Charitable Bingo Association. "The non-profits just cannot compete with the for-profit gaming industry unless they're given the opportunity to conduct their gaming the same way.... Bingo needs to reinvent itself."

Profits for charities from bingo and other gaming dropped about 13% from 2001 to 2003 before rebounding about 1% in 2004 in about 30 states that track the business, says Mary Magnuson, legal counsel for the Minnesota-based National Association of Fundraising Ticket Manufacturers. "Clearly, the commercial gambling is having an impact," Magnuson says. Other factors that have diminished bingo's appeal are smoking bans that prevent players from lighting up and the game's image as a pastime for seniors, she says.

Bingo's decline coincides with the explosion of legalized gambling across the USA in the past 15 years. States have sanctioned commercial casinos and expanded lotteries to raise revenue and avoid hiking taxes to pay for services. More recently, states such as Iowa and Louisiana have begun allowing slot machines at racetracks. Utah and Hawaii are the only states that ban gambling.

Steps states are taking or considering to help charity gaming:

- Last week, Minnesota began allowing several bingo halls to link up for a single game via the Internet, potentially increasing the jackpot from hundreds to thousands of dollars.
- Michigan will require bingo halls to meet minimum appearance standards by Oct. 1 to make them more appealing to patrons.
- In Pennsylvania, a bill that would double the amount of bingo prize money groups can award in a single day was approved by the state House of Representatives last year and awaits action in the Senate.

Reviving bingo's fortunes is vital to non-profit groups, advocates say. "In many instances, it is (their) primary source of money," Magnuson says. "What happens to the volunteer fire department if they can't raise money through bingo?"

—Charisse Jones

Above: Seniors play charity bingo at a community center in the Midwest.

Charitable gambling has struggled to keep up with all these changes. Young people tend to dismiss bingo as too slow and boring. As a result, many nonprofits are looking toward technology to reignite interest in bingo. Electronic bingo, Internet bingo, and huge jackpots are just a few ideas that supporters hope will keep charitable gambling alive.

But some argue that the technological changes to charitable gambling only blur the legal line. They claim that innovations create a slippery slope that encourages gambling to grow unchecked. For example, bingo hall operators constantly try to expand the definition of bingo. If it's legal for players to use physical cards and markers, why shouldn't electronic cards and markers be legal? And if electronic cards and markers are legal, why limit players to the pace of a game in a particular place? Why not allow video terminals where players can compete against virtual opponents much more quickly?

Above: This California casino offers electronic bingo machines.

> **"There's not a problem with charitable gaming if it's run the way it was designed to run. We think that it's getting a little out of control."**
>
> **—RICK KALM,** EXECUTIVE DIRECTOR, MICHIGAN GAMING CONTROL BOARD, 2009

Above: Legislators examined this electronic bingo terminal, which is very similar in appearance to an electronic slot machine.

The problem with electronic bingo, some say, is that it's essentially just a dressed-up slot machine. The game may technically be bingo, but the spirit of the game has disappeared. To some, the distinction is unimportant. They don't see how one form of gambling could be better or worse than another. To others, electronic bingo represents a dangerous shift. If terminals that are essentially slot machines are okay, will true slot machines follow? What about table games such as blackjack? How long will it be before any non-profit can open a full-fledged casino? And as charitable gambling expands, who will regulate it? Who will prevent fraud and make sure that profits really go where they're supposed to go?

CHAPTER EIGHT

Going Digital: Online Gambling

T HE VAST MAJORITY OF AMERICANS CARED LITTLE about the January 15, 2007, news that the Federal Bureau of Investigation (FBI) had arrested two Canadian businessmen as they traveled through the United States. But the news sent shock waves through the U.S. community of online gamblers.

The arrests came just a few months after the U.S. Congress passed the Unlawful Internet Gambling Enforcement Act (UIGEA) of 2006. This law made it illegal to transfer funds into and out of online gaming sites. The two businessmen, John Lefebvre and Steve Lawrence, had founded a company called Neteller. Neteller is an e-wallet, a service that helps its customers move money into and out of online gambling sites. At the time, Neteller was the giant of the industry, handling about 80 percent of online gaming transactions. U.S. officials charged Lefebvre and Lawrence with money laundering, or disguising illegally

Left: Paradise Poker is an online gaming site owned by the British company Sportingbet. As of 2009, Sportingbet was one of the world's largest online gaming companies, operating sports betting and casino sites in addition to poker.

obtained funds so that they seem legal. And the government froze all Neteller's U.S. assets (money and property).

For online gamers, the news was devastating. They had lost their main means of transferring money online. And those who had funds with Neteller at the time had no access to that money. Neteller responded quickly and cooperated with the government. The company announced that it would no longer do business with U.S. customers. It promised to return their funds when the U.S. government allowed Neteller to do so. That meant a wait of months for nervous players, some of whom had thousands—or even tens of thousands—of dollars tied up in Neteller. Others worried that Neteller would hand over to U.S. officials personal and financial data identifying players who'd been involved in illegal gambling.

The arrests marked a new level of online gambling enforcement in the United States. Law enforcement agencies had, in gambling terms, raised the stakes.

Above: Neteller is part of the British company Neovia. The company provides e-wallet and credit card services to people in more than 160 countries. Users can use their accounts for mail-order and video-game purchases as well as gambling.

Above: A gambler logs on to PartyPoker, one of the first and most popular online gaming sites.

THE EARLY DAYS OF ONLINE GAMING

A new chapter in the history of gambling began in 1995 when the first online casinos, the Gaming Club and Intercasino, opened for business. It didn't take long for online gaming to catch on. In 1996 the first online sportsbook, Intertops, opened. The first Internet poker room, Planet Poker, followed in 1998. By then annual revenues for online gambling had topped one billion dollars. More than half the revenues came from U.S. players.

The industry grew steadily through the late 1990s and early 2000s. Most online gaming companies were located in small countries (most notably Antigua and Barbuda) with little or no gambling regulation. So the early years of online gambling were a bit like the Wild West. What laws existed were all but meaningless. Any player betting money online took the very real risk of being cheated.

As the industry matured and attracted more players, many companies flourished.

Neteller frozen funds' resolution may affect online gambling industry

From the Pages of USA TODAY

Payday has finally come for hundreds of thousands of U.S. customers whose money has been tied up for months in a beleaguered Internet money-transfer service popular among gamblers.

Under a deal reached with the U.S. Attorney's office in Manhattan last month, Neteller has begun to allow consumers access to their accounts following a months-long federal investigation.

So far, $70 million has been withdrawn.

The resolution of the longstanding case—watched closely in the gaming industry—could have far-reaching implications for consumers and law-enforcement officials trying to muzzle online gambling, which is illegal.

For U.S. customers, it's been a frenzied period for cashing out. Some 250,000 accounts with positive balances had been frozen since January, when Neteller halted operations in the USA after authorities arrested its Canadian founders, charging them with handling billions of dollars in illegal gambling proceeds. About two-thirds of Neteller's business came from the USA.

The company still does business in 160 countries. It's considering re-entering the U.S. market in non-gaming areas, Neteller spokesman Andrew Gilchrist says. During the federal probe of Neteller, FBI agent Neil Donovan said, funds were held in court as potential evidence.

The investigation is a big part of a nationwide crackdown against online gambling. A law signed by President Bush in October bans the use of credit cards, checks and electronic fund transfers for Internet gaming. Still, U.S. residents place more than half of all bets to major [online] casinos in an estimated $16.3 billion industry. However, most online gaming sites are based offshore, outside the reach of American law enforcement.

Neteller was the de facto payment processor for gambling transactions after PayPal dropped out of the U.S. gambling market in 2003 as part of a settlement with the federal government. PayPal, which is owned by eBay, offers payment services for gaming where it is legal, such as in Europe.

Money-transfer companies such as Neteller do business with financial institutions and merchants. But many also allow gambling companies to transfer money collected from U.S. gamblers to bank accounts outside the USA.

The feds' actions against Neteller have had the desired effect of forcing other payment processors, such as InstaDebit Services and Citadel Commerce, from the U.S. market.

Whether this deters Americans from making wagers online is another matter, industry experts say. Many will continue to use other payment-processing systems, money orders and cashier's checks.

A conspiracy charge against Neteller, which is publicly traded in London, will be dismissed after two years if it meets the conditions of its agreement. Neteller must forfeit $136 million, restore the $94 million in the accounts of U.S. residents, and admit to violating U.S. law, according to the deal.

Neteller's co-founders, Stephen Lawrence and John Lefebvre, have pleaded guilty to a charge of conspiracy to transfer funds with the intent to promote illegal gambling. They each face up to five years in prison on the charge.

"Our highest priority is to get funds back" to U.S. customers, Neteller CEO Ron Martin said in a video posted July 31 on YouTube. Neteller has notified U.S. members via e-mail, instructing them to sign onto their accounts at neteller.com to withdraw funds.

Customers can receive their money through an electronic transfer to their bank account or by check to their mailing address. Most are opting for the transfer, which takes about a day.

Neteller customers also are receiving a waiver release, in which they and Neteller agree not to sue each other, say customers who e-mailed copies of the release to *USA TODAY*.

Neteller customers [shouldn't be] concerned about criminal charges. says a former federal prosecutor. "As a general matter, the federal government's interest is in going after the bookmaker instead of the gambler," says Joseph DeMarco, an Internet and privacy attorney who used to be assistant U.S. Attorney in Manhattan.

—Jon Swartz

PartyGaming, on the strength of its popular PartyPoker site, became the first online gaming company to go public (sell its stock on a public stock market) in 2005. Online gambling was officially a big business.

Early on, governments could do little to curb online gaming. One way the U.S. government tried to crack down was by targeting the sources of funding for gaming sites. In 2006 Jim Leach, a U.S. representative from Iowa, introduced a bill to ban credit card companies from doing business with known online gambling operations. The proposed legislation proved unnecessary, as credit card companies complied on their own.

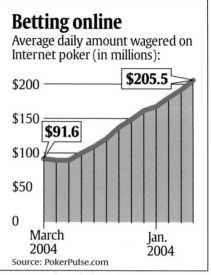

Betting online

Average daily amount wagered on Internet poker (in millions):

$205.5

$91.6

March 2004

Jan. 2004

Source: PokerPulse.com

By Joni Alexander, USA TODAY, 2005

"When I first introduced the legislation . . . the credit card companies were massively opposed," Leach said. "As time has gone on, they have figured out they are the losers. Even though they were making tidy

> " I think [online gambling is] really an explosion because you don't have to move out of your house. You can sit in your pajamas and lose everything you have. "
>
> **—ARNIE WEXLER,** A RECOVERING COMPULSIVE GAMBLER
> ● USA TODAY · MARCH 13, 2000

Above: Jeff Markley, a vice president at poker news and online gambling company Bluff Media, checks out several popular online poker sites. As laws about online gambling changed, the company covered the challenge to its online activities in its magazine, *Bluff.*

sums in transactions, when people can't pay back their transactions, the credit card companies have to pick it up."

As credit card companies realized the risks, most of them banned gambling transactions. But the move did little to curb online gaming. People found other ways to gamble on the Internet. They used financial tools such as wire transfers, debit cards, and e-wallets instead.

RAISING THE STAKES

Online gambling in the United States carried on basically unchecked throughout the late 1990s and early 2000s. Its legal status was very much in question. Did state laws cover online betting when it was carried through sites in other countries? That uncertain status changed in October 2006 with the Security and Accountability for Every Port Act (SAFE Port Act).

The SAFE Port Act introduced measures to protect U.S. ports from terrorism. It had almost universal support from Republicans and Democrats alike. At the last minute, lawmakers—mainly those who identified themselves

Above: President George W. Bush *(seated)* signs the SAFE Port Act in Washington, D.C., in 2006.

as Christian conservatives—added to it provisions completely unrelated to port security. These provisions made up the Unlawful Internet Gambling Enforcement Act of 2006. UIGEA joined the SAFE Port Act so late that many members of Congress never even read it, and the public had little chance to weigh in. Because port security was vital, few members of Congress dared vote against the bill. They feared doing so would be political suicide (would end their political careers).

On September 30, 2006, the act passed the House of Representatives 409–2 and passed the Senate unanimously. President George W. Bush signed it into law on October 13, 2006.

Within a few months, UIGEA halted players' ability to fund and retrieve money from online gambling accounts. The U.S. government threatened to punish large e-wallets such as Neteller and forced them to stop doing business with U.S. customers. Tens of thousands of U.S. players found their online funds frozen. Almost instantly, gaming sites such as PartyPoker stopped accepting U.S. players.

> " How dare you come into my house and tell me what I can and can't do on the Internet. . . . [The fight against UIGEA is] a cause for personal choice and freedom that I've always thought epitomizes what this country's about. "
>
> —**ALFONSE D'AMATO,** FORMER NEW YORK SENATOR AND CHAIR OF THE POKER PLAYERS ALLIANCE, 2009

Above: Former New York senator Alfonse D'Amato tosses a chip at his weekly card game. As chair of the Poker Players Alliance, he supported regulation of online gambling but not a complete ban.

Many people stood up to protest the law, claiming that the government had no right to decide what they could do in the privacy of their own homes. Others protested not the law but the way in which it passed, which many considered underhanded. The Poker Players Alliance and other groups lobbied hard against UIGEA.

Members of Congress also spoke out against the law. Massachusetts representative Barney Frank said, "The existing legislation is an inappropriate interference on the personal freedom of Americans and this interference should be undone." Frank and other lawmakers tried to overturn UIGEA, but they failed.

UIGEA dealt a severe blow to online gaming in the United States. But serious players eventually found loopholes in the law and various ways to skirt its limitations. UIGEA mainly restricts U.S. companies, not U.S. gamblers. The law does not apply to financial institutions based entirely outside the United States. As U.S. gamblers found these companies, online gaming in the

Above: Massachusetts representative Barney Frank tried to overturn UIGEA. He says that he himself does not gamble.

United States slowly revived—much to the chagrin of many state and local governments.

STATES TAKE ADDITIONAL STEPS

Some states tried to take matters into their own hands. Kentucky's governor, Steve Beshear, had campaigned on a promise to bring casinos to the state. In 2008 Beshear sought permission from Kentucky's judicial system to seize more than one hundred website names belonging to Internet gambling sites. Beshear wanted to shut them down. "We think [online gambling] creates a tremendous disadvantage for our legitimate, licensed and taxed gaming interests, and there are some damages [payments] that are due to the commonwealth [state] as a result," said Jennifer Brislin, spokesperson for the Kentucky Department of Justice.

In October 2008, a state circuit court granted Kentucky permission to seize the requested Web addresses. Opponents argued that the move violated property rights and free speech. In January 2009, the Kentucky Court of Appeals agreed. The court said that the seizures would have been legal only if Kentucky had first established that the sites' owners were using them to carry out illegal activities. The court also said that allowing the state government to seize website names indiscriminately would set a dangerous precedent.

In April 2009, Minnesota tried another approach: outright censorship. The Minnesota Department of Public Safety gave Internet service providers (ISPs) throughout the state a deadline to block access to about two hundred gambling and gambling-related websites. The state cited the Interstate

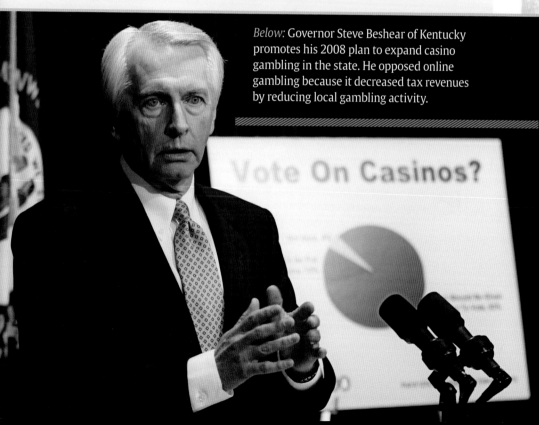

Below: Governor Steve Beshear of Kentucky promotes his 2008 plan to expand casino gambling in the state. He opposed online gambling because it decreased tax revenues by reducing local gambling activity.

Wire Act of 1961, a federal law banning the use of wire communications, such as phones, to place wagers. The order would block any Internet user in Minnesota from connecting to the gambling sites—and would also block the phone numbers associated with those sites. The measure would also lock e-wallet users out of their accounts.

"We are putting site operators and Minnesota online gamblers on notice and in advance," said John Willems, director of the state's Alcohol and Gambling Enforcement Division. "State residents with online escrow [e-wallet] accounts should be aware that access to their accounts may be jeopardized and their funds in peril."

The Interstate Wire Act of 1961

The legality of online gambling in the United States is a hotly debated issue. Federal and state governments seeking to outlaw online gambling have pointed to a 1961 law that banned the use of wire communications—which then mainly meant phones—for sports betting. The Interstate Wire Act of 1961 (also called the Federal Wire Act) was intended to curb sports betting operations among organized crime groups.

Supporters of legalized Internet gambling argue that the Federal Wire Act does not apply to online gaming. The act specifically refers to sports betting and betting done by phone. They point to a 2002 ruling in the U.S. Court of Appeals for the Fifth Circuit. The court ruled that the Federal Wire Act is clear in its intent, as evidenced by the phrase *sporting event or contest*. The act repeats this phrase several times.

Critics of the measure questioned Minnesota's motivation in trying to shut down online gaming. State officials admitted that they didn't know how many of Minnesota's residents took part in online gaming. But they pointed out that the poker room attached to a racetrack in Shakopee, Minnesota, had seen a significant drop in recent years. Officials blamed this drop on increased online gaming. Minnesota officials, like those in Kentucky, believed out-of-state online gambling establishments harmed Minnesota businesses and state revenues.

"The fact is, online poker is not illegal," said Matt Werden, PPA's Minnesota director. "It's not criminal, and it cannot be forcibly blocked by a state authority looking to score some political points [with Minnesotans worried about the state's economy]," he continued. "We see headlines like this coming from communist China but never expect that it could happen here in Minnesota."

Above: Minnesota state officials pointed to online gaming as one cause of declining business in the poker room at the Canterbury Downs racetrack in Shakopee, Minnesota.

> " The [Minnesota] Department of Public Safety has to have better things to do with their time than to go after a college kid in his dorm room or some guy sitting in his basement spending a couple of hours playing online poker. Demanding that a private-sector Internet service provider block access to websites is not a proper function of our state government. "

—MINNESOTA STATE REPRESENTATIVE PAT GAROFALO, 2009

Some legal experts question Minnesota's interpretation of a law written long before the Internet existed. "I think this is a very problematic and significant misreading of the statute," said John Morris, general counsel (attorney) at the Center for Democracy and Technology in Washington, D.C.

Ultimately, the state bowed to pressure from critics. In June 2009, state officials lifted the order it had given to ISPs. Some state officials vowed that the battle wasn't over, however.

A BETTER APPROACH?

The U.S. government's intolerance of online gambling has been largely ineffective. Meanwhile, the United Kingdom, Australia, and other countries have adopted another strategy. These countries have conceded that online gaming bans simply won't work. Rather than waste resources trying to enforce harsh, problematic bans, they have invested resources in legalizing Internet gambling.

Proponents of legalized, regulated online gaming

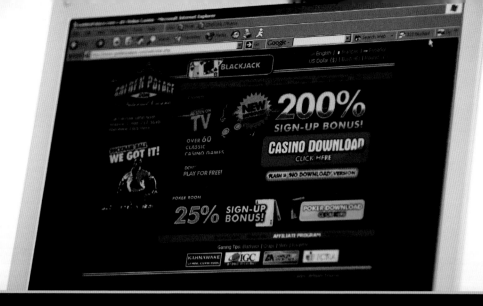

Above: Online gambling is legal in the United Kingdom, but the government created tighter controls on online gambling after a national charity publicized the ease with which children could sign on to this and other online gaming sites.

point to the United Kingdom's Gambling Act 2005 as a model for the United States to follow. The Gambling Act 2005 spells out the licensing and regulation of online gambling. It also sets up a national gaming commission to protect the consumer.

This approach has several benefits. By working with gaming sites, governments retain some measure of control over how the sites run. Governments can establish and standardize safeguards against gambling by minors, for example.

According to an informal 2009 *U.S. News and World Report* poll, 98 percent of respondents supported the legalization of online gambling. Players in countries with legal, regulated online gaming can safely and easily move money in and out of the gaming sites. They have no need to hide their gambling as U.S. players do. The need to hide can lead to intricate, risky—and illegal—money-laundering schemes. Supporters of legalization argue that the online gambling ban simply draws players from one illegal activity to another.

Politician favors legalizing online gambling

From the Pages of
USA TODAY

At a time when most economic news is bleak, maybe we can take a tip from England, and the British Open bets that will be placed this week with that nation's legal bookmakers. There, winnings are easily taxed. Here? More and more sports wagering is conducted online, through offshore websites.

"We gamble billions of dollars in this country, and the Internal Revenue Service doesn't get a dime," Lee Trevino tells ESPN.com in a story from the Open at Southport, England. "Instead, they spend millions of dollars trying to catch these people."

Rep. Jim A. McDermott, D-Wash., is trying to change that, in legislation introduced this week that would legalize, regulate and tax online gambling. Based on research by PricewaterhouseCoopers, McDermott believes as much as $40 billion could be generated over the next 10 years.

He also believes the hard economic times will help open minds of his colleagues in Congress to legalizing online gambling. "I don't think there could be a better time," McDermott says. The online gaming industry generally supports such legislation, believing regulated gambling would attract more customers.

"What's going on now is around the edges of legality in various countries of the world, and (bettors) aren't sure where their money is going," McDermott says.

McDermott likens the current betting environment to the "criminal structure" that accompanied Prohibition. He also finds attitudes [against] gambling outdated. Says McDermott: "If we can take revenue from horse racing we certainly can take revenue from online."

—Tom Weir

And when online gambling is legal, governments can tax the sites' profits. Economists at PricewaterhouseCoopers, a global financial services company, estimated in 2009 that the regulation and taxation of online gaming could generate more than fifty billion dollars in tax revenue for the U.S. government over ten years. Many suggest that revenues could be even higher, since the economists made their estimates based on the amount of online gaming taking place in the United States in 2009. Most of this gaming was illegal. If the United States legalized and regulated online gaming, more people would take part and revenues would rise accordingly.

ATTRACTING THE WRONG CROWD?

Opponents of legalization say increased participation is a good reason not to legalize Internet gaming. The more people gamble, the more people become addicted.

One of the biggest problems with online gambling, critics say, is its accessibility and appeal to young people. For many young adults, online gaming is a way of life. Stories of college students using tuition money for Internet gambling on poker, sports, or casino games are far too common.

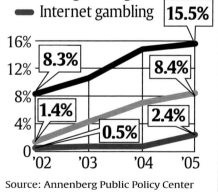

Gambling at college

Percentage of college students who say they take part in various kinds of gambling, including playing the lottery, in an average week:

- All gambling
- Card gambling
- Internet gambling

15.5%

8.3%

8.4%

1.4%

0.5%

2.4%

16%

12%

8%

4%

0

'02   '03   '04   '05

Source: Annenberg Public Policy Center

By Joni Alexander, USA TODAY, 2005

It's always poker night on campus

From the Pages of USA TODAY

Every Sunday at 6 P.M., coast to coast, more than a thousand college students go online to compete for scholarship money in the qualifying rounds of a national poker tournament. Others play the hot poker game Texas Hold'em in all-night tournaments, at campus fundraisers, in dorm rooms with friends, or increasingly, on the Internet.

Poker, once a pastime for cowboys in Wild West saloons but now a cash cow for cable TV, is at the forefront of a gambling craze that has swept colleges nationwide. "The popularity of poker is absolutely phenomenal," says Elizabeth George, chief executive of the North American Training Institute, which specializes in dealing with problems of youth gambling. Edward Looney, executive director of the Council on Compulsive Gambling of New Jersey, attributes poker's surge to its glamorization on TV shows and to the accessibility of the Internet and credit cards.

Half of college men say they have gambled on cards at least once a month this year, up from 45% in 2004, according to a study released in September by the University of Pennsylvania's Annenberg Public Policy Center. About 15% of them played at least once a week in 2005, up from 2% in 2002. Only 1.6% of college women said they played weekly this year.

Card players are more likely than other gamblers to go online, the report says. It cites a fivefold increase in weekly Internet betting since 2002.

Experts say poker's popularity is the result of a trend toward greater acceptance of gambling in the USA—from horse racing in the 1930s to bingo, lotteries, riverboats, Indian casinos and the Internet. Toy stores now sell poker sets, and public colleges offer courses and even majors on gambling and casinos.

"Gambling has become a more mainstream activity," says Dan Romer, director of the Annenberg survey. He calls it a "worrisome" trend. "Younger people are more prone to addiction than older people. Some kids who play will get hooked."

The survey found that 54.5% of young people who gambled weekly reported at least one problem, including overspending or social withdrawal. It says card players reported more problems than other gamblers. Of those

Above: LeHigh University student Greg Hogan arrives at a court appearance in 2006. He pleaded guilty to robbing a bank to pay his online poker debts.

who gambled at least once a month, 10% said they owe people money as a result.

This month in Allentown, Pa., Lehigh University student Greg Hogan robbed a bank to pay off a $5,000 debt incurred through online poker, according to his attorney, John Waldron. Hogan, 19, appears an unlikely bandit. President of his sophomore class and son of a Baptist minister, he also played second-chair cello in the university orchestra and worked in the chaplain's office.

But Waldron says Hogan got addicted to poker in college and started borrowing money. "It just got him in the hole. It overwhelmed him," Waldron says. "He made a decision that just wasn't him."

"We're seeing a lot of good kids with gambling problems," Looney says. He estimates that 5% of gamblers develop serious problems. Those seeking help are "anxious, depressed—they feel alone, isolated," says Dennis Heitzmann, a psychologist who has been director of counseling services at Pennsylvania State University for 20 years.

Many counseling centers are ill-equipped to deal with gambling addiction, says Clayton Neighbors, a psychiatry professor at the University of Washington. He says the problem is generally less understood than alcohol or drug abuse. He says college students, away from home for the first time, are vulnerable. "They are in that period where they're willing to experiment with almost anything," he says.

"We're not communicating adequately the risks," says Keith Whyte, executive director of the National Council on Problem Gambling. "Government, which typically deals with these issues, has a conflict of interest," he says, because states profit from gambling ventures such as casinos and lotteries.

—Wendy Koch

Above: As children gain increased access to and knowledge of technology, it becomes easier for them to stumble into problems with online gambling.

Critics of online gambling say that many sites do little or nothing to verify that a player is of legal gambling age. Often a player must provide only credit card information. One study showed that one-third of all online gaming sites had loopholes that would allow a minor to play easily. Some underage gamblers don't even realize that they're breaking the law. They may believe that since Internet gambling is available to them, it must be okay for them to play.

Underage gambling is a serious problem. Teens are up to three times more likely than adults to become compulsive gamblers. Furthermore, they often don't fully understand the consequences of their actions. For example, in 2004 a seventeen-year-old New Jersey boy stole his father's credit card to play online poker. The boy lost money and then gambled more in an attempt to win back his losses. He ran up a ten-thousand-dollar debt before his father discovered what had happened. Compulsive gambling is a problem likely to follow a teen into adulthood. High school- and college-age youths can permanently damage their financial futures. That, critics say, is one of the greatest dangers of online gaming.

EPILOGUE

The Future

RECENT DECADES HAVE SEEN WIDESPREAD CHANGES in the landscape of gambling in the United States. From the emergence of state-sponsored gaming and Indian gaming to the explosion of online gaming, gamblers have more legal options than ever before.

The tendency in the latter half of the twentieth century and the beginning of the twenty-first century has been for less stringent restrictions on gambling. States have embraced gambling as a source of much-needed revenue. In fact, many states would have trouble balancing a budget without gambling. Some have called for lawmakers to step back and slow down, but many others believe that the choice to gamble should be up to the individual, not the government.

Online gambling, more than any other form, may drive the future of gambling legislation. Lawmakers still do not have a firm grasp on exactly what people should and should not be able to do online. Nor do lawmakers know how state and local laws might apply to the very international medium of the Internet. Will U.S. lawmakers continue trying to

Left: In 2008 the line to buy tickets to a new Idaho lottery game snaked out the door of a convenience store in the city of Nampa.

stifle online gambling in all its forms? Or will they eventually pursue regulation and taxation? How will they protect generations of future kids who grow up in a world where, with a little effort, just about anyone can place a wager anytime, from the comfort of their own home?

WHAT IS FAIR?

The debate over the legalization of gambling is complicated. Both sides present many compelling arguments. How should a government weigh the rights of the individual against the overall good of society?

The U.S. Declaration of Independence clearly spells out the rights of Americans to life, liberty, and the pursuit of

Above: Already a successful poker player at the age of nineteen, Canadian college student Aaron Armstrong taught himself how to minimize his gambling risks. He limited the time he spent at online gambling and stopped after losing a certain amount.

happiness. For many, gambling is a way to unwind and enjoy themselves—to pursue happiness. The vast majority of gamblers wager responsibly.

But for a small percentage of people, gambling is a dangerous, destructive force—one from which they aren't able to easily escape. Their inability to control their gambling urges can damage their lives and the lives of people close to them. When that happens, everyone pays a price.

What is fair? How can the United States protect the rights of all without putting some people in danger? How should laws ensure the greatest possible benefit to U.S. society?

There are no easy answers. Outlawing all forms of gambling is unrealistic, while legalizing all forms could be dangerous. Any middle ground is subject to claims of unfairness. There's only one safe bet when it comes to legalized gambling: the debate isn't likely to disappear anytime soon.

TIMELINE

1542   England passes one of the first antigambling laws.

1729   France begins a royal lottery for municipal bondholders.

1776   The United States declares independence from Great Britain and sets up a lottery to help pay for the Revolutionary War effort.

1848   John Marshall discovers gold in California, setting off a gold rush and ushering in the Wild West period.

1919   Several members of the Chicago White Sox baseball team, in cahoots with professional gamblers, intentionally lose the World Series. The Black Sox scandal helps bring to light the dangers gambling presents to sports integrity. The U.S. government passes the Eighteenth Amendment prohibiting the sale, transportation, or manufacture of alcohol. Prohibition brings more anti-gambling laws nationwide.

1929   New York toy salesman Edwin Lowe discovers the game of beano at a Florida carnival and brings it back to New York. He renames the game bingo and starts a new gambling craze.

1933   The Prohibition era ends.

1934   Americans play about ten thousand bingo games per week—both legally and illegally—in the United States.

1940s   Las Vegas becomes the gambling capital of the United States as lavish new hotels and casinos draw many tourists.

1951   Thirty-five college basketball players are accused of point-shaving, a scandal that ruins basketball careers and shuts down the University of Kentucky's basketball program for a full season.

1961 The U.S. Congress passes the Federal Wire Act to prevent interstate sports betting among organized crime groups.

1964 New Hampshire resurrects the idea of state-sponsored lotteries by starting the New Hampshire sweepstakes.

1974 The modern system of state-sponsored lotteries starts in New York. Thirty-five states have legalized bingo for fund-raising purposes.

1980 The American Psychiatric Association formally recognizes compulsive gambling as an impulse control disorder.

1988 Congress passes the Indian Gaming Regulatory Act, acknowledging the right of Indian tribes to conduct gaming on tribal lands.

1989 Major League Baseball bans Pete Rose for life as a result of his betting on baseball.

1990s Indian gaming rapidly expands. As state-sponsored racetracks struggle to stay afloat, many states pass laws allowing casino-style games on racetrack grounds. Some states legalize riverboat casinos.

1992 Powerball sells its first tickets. Powerball soon becomes the largest multistate lottery in the United States. The Professional and Amateur Sports Protection Act outlaws sports betting in forty-six states.

1995 The first online casinos, the Gaming Club and Intercasino, open for business.

1998 The first online poker room, Planet Poker, opens.

2003 Amateur Chris Moneymaker wins the World Series of Poker, setting off a poker boom both online and in live card rooms.

2004 California governor Arnold Schwarzenegger makes headlines by claiming that the state's Native American tribes "are ripping us off." Californians vote down Proposition 70, which would allow the expansion of Indian casinos.

2006 Congress passes the Unlawful Internet Gambling Enforcement Act of 2006, which makes the funding of online gambling accounts illegal.

2007 U.S. officials arrest Neteller founders John Lefebvre and Steve Lawrence while the two men travel through the United States. Officials charge the men with money laundering. The U.S. government freezes all Neteller's U.S. assets, sending shock waves through the online gambling community.

2008 Kentucky courts rule that the state has the right to seize the website names of online gambling sites. The Kentucky Court of Appeals later overturns the decision.

2009 Minnesota officials order the state's Internet service providers to block online gambling sites but later backs off from this demand due to public outrage over perceived censorship. A Pennsylvania judge rules that poker is a game of skill and, therefore, that state's antigambling laws do not apply to it.

GLOSSARY

abstinence: the complete avoidance of an activity, such as gambling

bankruptcy: a legal declaration of the inability to pay one's debts

casting lots: an ancient form of gambling. Many ancient texts, including the Bible, mention casting lots—but the mechanics of the activity are unknown.

chasing losses: a behavior in which a gambler bets more and more money in hopes of winning back what he or she has already lost

escrow: an arrangement in which a party holds and transfers money between a customer and a service

e-wallet: an escrow service that allows a player to transfer money to and from online gambling sites

money laundering: concealing the source of illegally obtained money

point-shaving: intentionally reducing the margin of victory in a sports competition

precedent: a legal decision that can influence future decisions

racino: a racetrack that offers casino-style games, such as slot machines

sovereign: independent; having the right to self-government

sportsbook: a gambling agent or establishment that takes bets on sporting events

Texas Hold'em: the most popular variant of poker

SOURCE NOTES

7   Bruce Lambert and Valerie Cotsalas, "Bookkeeper Admits Embezzling $2.3 Million for Lottery Habit," *New York Times,* August 24, 2006, http://query .nytimes.com/gst/fullpage.html?res=9E0DE4DB133EF937A1575BC0A9609 C8B63 (July 12, 2009).

7   Ibid.

7   Associated Press, "Lottery Addict Screams at Judge for Jail Sentence," *WCBS TV,* September 27, 2006, http://wcbstv.com/watercooler/Lottery.Long.Island.2 .238324.html (July 12, 2009).

10 Interdicasterial Commission of Cardinals and Bishops, "Catechism of the Catholic Church," *The Vatican Archives,* October 11, 1992, http://www.vatican .va/archive/ccc_css/archive/catechism/p3s2c2a7.htm (June 30, 2009).

16 Dennis Meredith, "Gambling Monkeys Give Insight into Neural Machinery of Risk," *Bio-Medicine,* August 22, 2005, http://news.bio-medicine.org/ biology-news-3/Gambling-monkeys-give-insight-into-neural-machinery-of- risk-10425-1 (June 11, 2009).

19 Gaius Suetonius Tranquillus, "De Vita Caesarum," *Project Gutenberg,* 121, http://www.gutenberg.org/etext/6400 (June 30, 2009).

19 L. C. Thomas, *Games, Theory, and Applications* (Mineola, NY: Dover Publications, 2003), 223.

24 Al Neuharth, "Super Bowl Bettors Ignore Tough Times," *USA Today,* January 30, 2009.

25 Thomas Jefferson, "Thomas Jefferson on Politics and Government," *Thomas Jefferson Digital Archive,* 2001, http://etext.virginia.edu/jefferson/quotations/ jeff1320.htm (June 30, 2009).

36 James Renner, "The Murder of Joseph Kupchik," *Cleveland Free Times,* January 10, 2007, http://www.freetimes.com/stories/14/38/the-murder-of-joseph- kupchik (July 12, 2009).

45 "New Treatment for Patients Struggling with Pathological Gambling," *Medical News Today,* February 2, 2006, http://www.medicalnewstoday.com/ articles/36991.php (July 12, 2009).

46 Monica Yant Kinney, "For Gambling Addict, N.J. List Is a Loser," *Philadelphia Inquirer,* March 15, 2009, http://www.philly.com/inquirer/opinion/20090315_ Monica_Yant_Kinney__For_gambling_addict__N_J__list_is_a_loser.html (July 12, 2009).

52 Martin Bashir and Sara Holmberg, "Powerball Winner Says He's Cursed," *ABC News,* April 6, 2007, http://abcnews.go.com/2020/Story?id=3012631&page=1 (July 12, 2009).

57 Steve Levin, "Poverty Leads to Playing Lottery, Study Says," *Pittsburgh Post-Gazette,* July 25, 2008.

57 Dennis Cauchon, "More States Roll the Dice on Slots," *USA Today,* January 10, 2008.

60 Patrick McMahon, "Gambling Bug Bites Needy States; Expansion Offers Tax Revenue, Jobs, but Some Warn of Overabundance," *USA Today,* August 29, 2002.

66 Greg Stumbo, "States Deserve a Cut," *USA Today,* February 9, 2009.

71 Chet Barfield, "'Fair Share' Depends on Who's Asked," *SignOnSanDiego.com,* October 10, 2004, http://www.signonsandiego.com/news/politics/20041010-9999-1n10rich.html (June 25, 2009).

72 Ibid.

78 Anahad O'Connor, "Rise in Income Improves Children's Behavior," *New York Times,* October 21, 2003.

79 Kate Spilde, "Indian Gaming in North Dakota: Resisting the Exodus," *National Indian Gaming Association,* November 2000, http://www.indiangaming.org/library/articles/north-dakota.shtml (July 12, 2009).

80 MacNeil/Lehrer Productions, "The Indian Gaming Issue," *The Online NewsHour Forum,* March 4, 1997, http://www.pbs.org/newshour/forum/march97/gambling_3-3.html (July 1, 2009).

80 Janell Ross and Clay Carey, "Payout or Pride, More Claim Indian Heritage," *USA Today,* September 12, 2008.

86 Tom Weir, "Online Sports Betting Spins out of Control; Ease of Use Attracts Young People, Athletes to Illegal Gambling," *USA Today,* August 22, 2003.

89 Chad Millman, "Behind the Bets," *ESPN: The Magazine,* March 10, 2009, http://sports.espn.go.com/espnmag/story?id=3968082 (July 1, 2009).

97 Michael McCarthy, "Vegas Makes Play for Team; Mayor Leading Push to Lure Big-League Franchise to Desert Says Don't Bet against Sin City," *USA Today,* November 30, 2005.

100 Steve DiMeglio, "Poker Pros, Fans, Going All In," *USA Today,* July 27, 2006.

102 Marco R. della Cava, "Poker at an Early Age: Not Just Another Teen Fad; With Some Parents Even Supporting Kids' Poker Parties, Addiction Experts Wonder Whether Stakes Are Too High," *USA Today,* December 21, 2004.

105 Gary Rotstein, "Legal Status of Poker: Is it a Game of Skill or Chance?" *Pittsburgh Post-Gazette,* March 1, 2009, http://www.post-gazette.com/pg/09060/952256-455.stm (July 12, 2009).

105 Rich Cholodofsky, "Judge Denies Request to Return Poker Cash," *Pittsburgh Tribune-Review,* October 10, 2007, http://www.pittsburghlive.com/x/ pittsburghtrib/news/westmoreland/s_531820.html (July 12, 2009).

106 Haley Hintze, "Pennsylvania Court Rules Poker a Game of Skill," *Poker News,* January 20, 2009, http://www.pokernews.com/news/2009/01/pennsylvania -court-rules-poker-skill-game-1035.htm (July 12, 2009).

112 David Johnston, "The Dark Side of Charity Gambling," *CNNMoney,* October 1, 1993, http://money.cnn.com/magazines/moneymag/moneymag_ archive/1993/10/01/88323/index.htm (July 12, 2009).

117 Joe Abfalter, "Charity Texas Hold'em and Controversy," *Michigan Card Player,* February 16, 2009, http://michigancardplayer.com/charity-texas-holdem- and-controversy (July 12, 2009).

124 Chris Jenkins, "Caught in Gambling's Web; Colleges Fear Students Easy Targets for Internet Sports Betting Sites," *USA Today,* March 13, 2000.

125 Tom Weir, "Online Sports Betting Spins out of Control; Ease of Use Attracts Young People, Athletes to Illegal Gambling," *USA Today,* August 22, 2003.

127 Frederic J. Frommer, "The Influence Game: Drawing to an Online Straight," *Safe and Secure Internet Gambling Initiative,* April 20, 2009, http://www .safeandsecureig.org/news/news_articles/09-04-20_AP.html (July 12, 2009).

128 Jennifer Newell, "Poker & Politics: A Vital Relationship Whether We Like It or Not," *Bluff,* November 2008, 98.

128 Brian Krebs, "Kentucky Tests State's Reach against Online Gambling," *Washington Post,* October 8, 2008, http://www.washingtonpost.com/wp-dyn/ content/article/2008/10/08/AR2008100802870.html (July 12, 2009).

130 Paul Walsh, "New Tactic in War on Online Gambling," *Star Tribune,* April 29, 2009, http://www.startribune.com/local/43985257.html?elr=KArksLckD8EQ DUoaEyqyP4O:DW3ckUiD3aPc:_Yyc:aUUI (July 12, 2009).

131 Advanced Global Applications, "Minnesota to Block Online Gambling; Poker Players Alliance Blasts Move," *PokerPages.com,* April 30, 2009, http://www .pokerpages.com/poker-news/news/minnesota-to-block-online-gambling- poker-players-alliance-blasts-move-31627.htm (July 12, 2009).

132 OG Paper.com, "Minnesota Online Gambling Ban under Fire from Legislature," *OG Paper,* May 5, 2009, http://www.ogpaper.com/news/Minnesota-online- gambling-050509.html (July 12, 2009).

132 Associated Press, "State Tries to Block Online Gaming," *KSTP.com,* April 29, 2009, http://kstp.com/news/stories/S904722.shtml?cat=206 (July 12, 2009).

SELECTED BIBLIOGRAPHY

Aasved, Mikal J. *The Sociology of Gambling.* Springfield, IL: Charles C. Thomas, 2003.

Eades, John M. *Gambling Addiction: The Problem, the Pain, and the Path to Recovery.* Ann Arbor, MI: Servant Publications, 2003.

Evans, Rod L., and Mark Hance, eds. *Legalized Gambling: For and Against.* Peru, IL: Open Court, 1998.

Haugen, David. *Legalized Gambling.* New York: Facts on File, 2006.

Haugen, David, and Susan Musser, eds. *Gambling.* Detroit: Thomson Gale, 2007.

Kredell, Matthew. "Online Poker's Past, Present, and Future." *Bluff,* November 2008, 108.

Light, Steven Andrew, and Kathryn R. L. Rand. *Indian Gaming and Tribal Sovereignty: The Casino Compromise.* Lawrence: University Press of Kansas, 2005.

Mason, W. Dale. *Indian Gaming: Tribal Sovereignty and American Politics.* Norman: University of Oklahoma Press, 2000.

Newell, Jennifer. "Poker and Politics: A Vital Relationship, Whether We Like It or Not." *Bluff,* November 2008, 96.

Rand, Kathryn R. L., and Steven Andrew Light. *Indian Gaming Law and Policy.* Durham, NC: Carolina Academic Press, 2006.

Saunders, Carol Silverman. *Straight Talk about Teenage Gambling.* New York: Facts on File, 1999.

Schwartz, David G. *Roll the Bones: The History of Gambling.* New York: Gotham Books, 2006.

Thompson, William Norman. *Legalized Gambling: A Reference Handbook.* Santa Barbara, CA: ABC-CLIO, 1997.

Vogel, J. Phillip. *Internet Gambling: How to Win Big Online Playing Bingo, Poker, Slots, Lotto, Sports Betting and Much More.* New York: Black Dog and Leventhal, 2006.

ORGANIZATIONS TO CONTACT

American Gaming Association (AGA)
1299 Pennsylvania Avenue NW, Suite 1175
Washington, DC 20004
202-552-2675
http://www.americangaming.org
AGA's goal is to create a better understanding of the gaming
entertainment industry. It does this by bringing facts about the
industry to the general public, to elected officials, and to the media
through education and advocacy.

Center for Gaming Research
4505 Maryland Parkway
Box 457010
Las Vegas, NV 89154-7010
702-895-2242
http://gaming.unlv.edu
The Center for Gaming Research, located at the University of Nevada in
Las Vegas, is a hub for the scholarly analysis of gambling and gaming
issues.

Gamblers Anonymous (GA)
P.O. Box 17173
Los Angeles, CA 90017
213-386-8789
http://www.gamblersanonymous.org
GA is a support organization for problem gamblers who wish to gain
control over their urges to gamble.

Institute for the Study of Gambling and Commercial Gaming
1664 N. Virginia Street MS/0025
Reno, NV 89557
775-784-1442
http://www.unr.edu/gaming
This institute, located at the University of Nevada in Reno, promotes
the study of the issues that surround commercial gambling.

National Center for Responsible Gaming (NCRG)
1299 Pennsylvania Avenue NW, Suite 1175
Washington, DC 20004
202-552-2689
http://www.ncrg.org
NCRG is devoted to funding research to increase understanding of pathological and youth gambling and to find effective methods of treatment for the disorder. This charitable organization is affiliated with the American Gaming Association.

National Council on Problem Gambling (NCPG)
730 11th Street NW, Suite 601
Washington, DC 20001
202-547-9204
http://www.ncpgambling.org
NCPG raises public awareness of problem and pathological gambling, ensures treatment for those in need, and supports research into problem gambling.

Poker Players Alliance (PPA)
1325 G Street NW, Suite 500
Washington, DC 20005
888-448-4772
http://pokerplayersalliance.org
PPA is a nonprofit membership organization composed of online and offline poker players. Its mission is to establish laws that provide poker players with secure, safe, and regulated places to play.

Stop Predatory Gambling Foundation
100 Maryland Avenue NE, Room 311
Washington, DC 20002
202-567-6996
http://www.ncalg.org
This group was formerly called the National Coalition Against Legalized Gambling. It compiles information on the adverse personal, social, economic, and public health impacts of gambling and disseminates the information to citizens and policy makers at the local, state, and national levels.

FURTHER READING

BOOKS

Bayer, Linda N. *Out of Control: Gambling and Other Impulse-Control Disorders.* Philadelphia: Chelsea House, 2001.
This illustrated title, developed in consultation with the American Psychiatric Press (APP), is written for young adults. It discusses the history of, causes and effects of, and treatments for compulsive gambling.

Beckelman, Laurie. *Gambling.* New York: Crestwood House, 1999.
The author presents gambling scenarios and questions to help readers gauge the impact of gambling on their lives.

Hjelmeland, Andy. *Legalized Gambling: Solution or Illusion?* Minneapolis: Twenty-First Century Books, 1998.
This book gives a historical overview of gambling and the law. It also presents a discussion of modern problems and laws associated with gambling.

Kallen, Stuart A., ed. *Indian Gaming.* Farmington, MI: Greenhaven Press, 2006.
This title, part of Greenhaven's At Issue series, discusses the pros and cons of Indian gaming and presents topics in a balanced fashion. Contributors include psychiatrists, activists, and more.

Saunders, Carol Silverman. *Straight Talk about Teenage Gambling.* New York: Facts on File, 1999.
Saunders discusses the psychology behind gambling and gambling addictions. She focuses on the impact of gambling on teens, who are especially vulnerable to its problems.

Savage, Jeff. *A Sure Thing? Sports and Gambling.* Minneapolis: Lerner Publications Company, 1997.
Savage looks at the relationship between sports and gambling and its pitfalls. He discusses professional gamblers, problem gamblers, treatments, and much more.

Stearman, Kaye. *Why Do People Gamble?* Austin, TX: Raintree Steck-Vaughn, 2001.
    Through case studies, facts and figures, and clear narrative, Stearman explores the reasons people are compelled to gamble and looks at the problems that can arise when the habit spins out of control.

Stewart, Gail B. *Gambling.* San Diego: Lucent Books, 2001.
    This title is packed with information about gambling and the controversy that often surrounds this activity. The author's straightforward approach provides lots of facts and figures about gambling in both the past and the present.

WEBSITES

American Gaming Association Fact Sheets
    http://www.americangaming.org/Industry/factsheets/index.cfm
    The American Gaming Association provides dozens of fact sheets on topics such as gambling history, Internet gambling, pathological gambling, and more.

Casino City Times: News
    http://www.casinocitytimes.com/news
    This independent directory includes links to the latest news in gambling, including legalization issues. A weekly newsletter highlights key gambling news stories.

Frontline: Easy Money
    http://www.pbs.org/wgbh/pages/frontline/shows/gamble
    PBS's *Frontline* includes a report on the gambling industry and its political connections. The report includes interviews, a timeline, and a discussion of odds. It also provides links to a variety of articles that discuss both sides of the debate on legalized gambling.

Mayo Clinic: Compulsive Gambling
    http://www.mayoclinic.com/health/compulsive-gambling/DS00443
    For a detailed look at compulsive gambling as a psychological disorder, check out the Mayo Clinic's website. The site includes a description of the disorder, symptoms and causes, and information on diagnosis and treatment.

INDEX

future of, 141–143; as inborn trait, 16–17; among macaque monkeys, 15–16; in 1900s, 27–33; number of gamblers in the United States, 37; reasons for, 38; societal costs of, 42–43; underage, 135–139

gambling, charitable. *See* charitable gambling

gambling, compulsive. *See* compulsive gambling

gambling, legalization of: in California, 26; charitable gambling, 109, 111, 115; and compulsive gambling, 11–12, 35–37, 58; economic arguments against, 10–11; economic incentives for, 62; fantasy sports, 104; future of, 142–143; horse racing, 28–29; in Las Vegas, 31; moral arguments against, 8–10; online, 33, 116–117, 130, 132–135; poker, 104–107; protests, 11; role of government, 12–13, 20, 23–26, 30, 53–58, 60, 132–135; sports betting, 88, 96

gambling, online. *See* online gambling

gambling, sports. *See* sports gambling

games of skill, 101–103; legal status, 104–107; poker, 99–101

Gaming Club, 121

Gandil, Arnold "Chick," 85–87

gold rush, 26

government, role of in gambling: in colonial era, 20; debate over, 12–13, 60; online, 132–135; state-sponsored lotteries, 23–26, 30, 53–58

Great Britain, 22–23, 133

Greece, ancient, 18

Harrington, Dan, 99

Hawaii, 56

Hawthorne Race Course, 29

Hogan, Greg, 137

Holthaus, Jean, 44

horse racing, 28–29, 32, 59

Hualapai tribe, 82–83

Illinois, 55, 61

Indiana, 68

Indian gaming. *See* Native American gaming

Indian Gaming Regulatory Act (IGRA), 30, 73–74

Intercasino, 121

Internet gambling. *See* online gambling

Interstate Wire Act of 1961, 130

Intertops, 121

Islam, 8, 9

Ivey, Phil, 106

Jackson, Andrew, 25

Jackson, "Shoeless" Joe, 85, 86

Jackson, Solomon, Jr., 32

jai alai, 88

Jefferson, Thomas, 24–25

Julius Caesar, 19

Kansas, 61, 68

keno halls, 59

Kentucky, 68, 128–129

Kephart, Jenny, 48–49

Kickapoo tribe, 77

Kupchik, Joseph, 35–37

Landis, Kenesaw Mountain, 86

Las Vegas, Nevada, 31

Lawrence, Steve, 119–120, 123

Lefebvre, John, 119–120, 123

Liubo, 18

lotteries: colonial, 22–23; cost, 58; early French, 21–22; early U.S. state-sponsored, 23–26, 30; lottery

PHOTO ACKNOWLEDGMENTS

The images in this book are used with the permission of: AP Photo/Shiho Fukada, pp. 4–5; AP Photo/Suffolk County District Attorneys Office, p. 6; © Ghaith Abdul-Ahad/Getty Images, p. 8; © Thad Allender/USA TODAY, p. 9; © Todd Plitt/USA TODAY, p. 10; AP Photo/James Crisp, p. 11; AP Photo/Christine Wetzel, p. 13; The Art Archive/Musée du Louvre Paris/Gianni Dagli Orti, pp. 14–15; © James Warwick/The Image Bank/Getty Images, p. 16; The Art Archive/ National Museum Karachi/Alfredo Dagli Orti, p. 17; © The Trustees of the British Museum/ Art Resource, NY, p. 18; © Mansell/Time & Life Pictures/Getty Images, p. 19; © MPI/Hulton Archive/Getty Images, pp. 20, 75; © AAAC/Topham/The Image Works, p. 21; © Jacques Boyer/Roger-Viollet/The Image Works, p. 22; The Granger Collection, New York, pp. 23, 25; © Rischgitz/Hulton Archive/Getty Images, p. 27; AP Photo, pp. 28, 30, 31, 86; AP Photo/Brett Flashnick, p. 32; © Karen Bleier/AFP/Getty Images, pp. 34–35; Press Association via AP Images, p. 36; © Monashee Frantz/RK Studio/Digital Vision/Getty Images, p. 37; © Steve Marcus/ USA TODAY, pp. 39, 101; AP Photo/Nati Harnik, p. 40; © Taro Yamasaki/Time & Life Pictures/ Getty Images, p. 41; AP Photo/Charlie Riedel, p. 44; AP Photo/Sara D. Davis, p. 46; © Robert Deutsch/USA TODAY, p. 47; © SuperStock/SuperStock, p. 49; AP Photo/Bob Bird, pp. 50–51; AP Photo/Jim Cole, p. 53; © Tim Dillon/USA TODAY, pp. 54, 128; AP Photo/Greg Campbell, p. 56; AP Photo/Bill Haber, p. 59; © Robert Hanashiro/USA TODAY, pp. 61, 80; © Bob Riha, Jr./ USA TODAY, pp. 63, 95; © Justin Sullivan/Getty Images, p. 64; AP Photo/Mary Ann Chastain, p. 65; AP Photo/Gail Burton, p. 67; AP Photo/Charlie Neibergall, p. 69; AP Photo/Denis Poroy, pp. 70–71; © Marisol Bello/USA TODAY, p. 72; © Richard Cummins/SuperStock, p. 73; © Jeff Haynes/AFP/Getty Images, p. 76; AP Photo/John P. Filo, p. 77; © H. Darr Beiser/USA TODAY, p. 78; AP Photo/Yes on 5, HO, p. 79; © Sarah Leen/National Geographic/Getty Images, p. 82; AP Photo/Ross D. Franklin, p. 83; Library of Congress, pp. 84–85 (LC-DIG-ggbain-25393); © Nocella/Hulton Archive/Getty Images, p. 87; AP Photo/J. Pat Carter, p. 88; AP Photo/Charles Knoblock, p. 90; AP Photo/John Swart, p. 91; AP Photo/Haraz N. Ghanbari, p. 94; AP Photo/ Jim Bryant, p. 97; AP Photo/Joe Cavaretta, pp. 98–99; © Leslie Smith, Jr./USA TODAY, p. 102; © Michael A. Schwarz/USA TODAY, p. 103; © Nathan Eldridge/Aurora/Getty Images, p. 105; © Eileen Blass/USA TODAY, pp. 106, 108–109; AP Photo/Pablo Martinez Monsivais, p. 107; © Morgan Collection/Hulton Archive/Getty Images, p. 110; © Margaret Bourke-White/Time & Life Pictures/Getty Images, p. 111; AP Photo/Bradley C. Bower, p. 112; AP Photo/Josh Reynolds, p. 113; © Matthias Clamer/Stone/Getty Images, p. 115; © Michael Allen Jones/ Sacramento Bee/ZUMA Press, p. 116; AP Photo/Harry Cabluck, p. 117; © Bruno Vincent/Getty Images, pp. 118–119; © Todd Strand/Independent Picture Service, p. 120; REUTERS/Toby Melville, p. 121; AP Photo/Ric Feld, p. 125; AP Photo/Charles Dharapak, p. 126; AP Photo/John Dunn, p. 127; AP Photo/Ed Reinke, p. 129; AP Photo/Jim Mone, p. 131; © Graeme Robertson/ Getty Images, p. 133; AP Photo/The Morning Call, Chuck Zovko, p. 137; © Tim Hall/Getty Images, p. 138; AP Photo/Idaho Press-Tribune, Mike Vogt, pp. 140–141; © The Toronto Star/ ZUMA Press, p. 142.

Front cover: © Gregor Schuster/Photographer's Choice/Getty Images.

ABOUT THE AUTHOR

Matt Doeden is a writer and editor who lives in New Prague, Minnesota. After earning degrees in journalism and psychology from Minnesota State University–Mankato, he began his career as a sports writer. Since then, he's spent nearly a decade writing and editing high-interest nonfiction, with more than fifty titles to his name on topics that range from extreme sports to military equipment to graphic novels. In the Sports Heroes and Legends series, his titles include *Tiger Woods, Dale Earnhardt Jr.,* and *Lance Armstrong.* His Motor Mania titles include *Crazy Cars* and *Lowriders.* Among his other LPG books are *Green Day* (Gateway Bio) and *Will Smith* (USA TODAY Lifeline Biographies).